# I Am The Crown

B.C. Raines

Published by Candy Publishing, LLC
www.candypublishing.net

ISBN: 978-0692152782

*Printed in the United States of America*

Editor, Jackie D. Rockwell

Cover Design, DK1 Promotions
www.dk1pro.com

# DEDICATION

To everyone who encouraged me to follow through with this book for the entire process.

To my village of women who instilled in me knowledge, wisdom, etiquette and values and provided genuine examples of women positively supporting women.

To my Mom and Dad for seeing something lovable in me before I saw it in myself.

To "my Creed" who teaches me so much about myself as he continues to "endure" my parenting journey.

To the memory of Mary Charles Burton, Ophelia H. Browder, Johnnie M. Sellers and Brenda T. Carter.

# I Am The Crown

## A Self-Discovery Guide

### for

## Girls and Women

# CONTENTS

www.sisterumatter.org

# I AM THE CROWN

# ABOUT THE BOOK

The goal of this book is to help you reclaim your Crown and all of the authority and influence that comes with it. Additionally, my hope is that this book will provide guidance regarding the proper fit of your reclaimed Crown, using it appropriately, and tips to maintain your Crown's beauty and eloquence. You know the up keep (maintenance) is just as important as the creation process.

Chapter 2 of this book will give you an opportunity to create a visual of your Crown. Although the Crown development navigated throughout this book is not tangible, the creation of a physical Crown, one that you can see, will be beneficial to use as a reminder of your internal Crown's beauty and uniqueness.

Since *I Am the Crown* is the title of the book, Sister, YOU Matter! had to be the theme (*although I have to admit I struggled with it being the title of the book*). This theme and the writing of this book have given birth to Sister U Matter!®,my outreach organization. The mission of Sister U Matter!® is to remind every woman being that she is essential to the existence of this world. It seeks to encourage and empower women to be the divine influences they were created to be in every facet of their lives.

The organization's goal is to inspire women beings to live their lives passionately and purposefully and to develop skills to assist with making wise and healthy life-sustaining choices, and to help a woman being know her value and worth. Sister, please know YOU Matter regardless of your current situation/circumstance,
 regardless of your past, regardless of your cultural
background...Sister, YOU Matter! Without you there would be an incredible void in this world. "Sister, YOU Matter!"will be

throughout and at the end of each chapter of this book to remind you that Sister, YOU Matter! For more information about the organization, visit the website at www.sisterumatter.org.

Lastly, this symbol will appear throughout this book. It represents what I call a "Crowning Moment." It will be your opportunity to be creative in your thinking and to explore what's needed to help you discover your self-worth, your Crown. Yes, you will have the opportunity to participate in this "Crowning" process. Now, are you ready? Say it again: "I Am the Crown!"

# INTRODUCTION

I want every woman being–girl, teen and adult–to know that there is no one and nothing more important in this world and in your life's plan than you.

I lived many years thinking that I did not matter, that I was not important, that I was unlovable, and that I was unnecessary to this world. (Let me clarify "unlovable." It was how I felt–and *not* about the actions of others in my life.) I felt like an insignificant being in this enormous world just waiting on someone else to choose me, to see my worth, to tell me my worth, to realize my potential and recognize my value.

I also felt like I was very different from everyone else and just didn't seem to fit in. I was not the popular girl in my school. I wasn't the prettiest girl; I wasn't the smartest girl either. I was not invited to join the popular cliques. I felt ordinary; I felt there was nothing spectacular about me. I was just trying to do well and be good to others–you know, "treat others the way I wanted to be treated."

Others told me I was smart and pretty. They said they could see my potential for success. But there was still this void inside me; this empty space that most times consumed me. I tried a multitude of things–lofty educational and career pursuits and unhealthy relationships, are a few that I'm not too ashamed to print in this book–to fill this emptiness; but everything I tried only provided a very temporary relief. Pretty soon, I would find that same emptiness consuming me all over again.

**Sister, YOU Matter!**

Sister, have you ever felt this way? I've talked with so many women from different cultures, ethnicities, religious affiliations and educational backgrounds, and for the most part, we all have communicated similar feelings of emptiness. Am I *enough*: good *enough*, smart *enough*, pretty *enough*, thin *enough*? Some have even admitted to thinking about or attempting to end their own lives.

*"Arguably, the biggest pop star in the world wasn't sure if she was good enough. She didn't think she looked right. There were a thousand things to her that seemed wrong...The Whitney I knew, despite her success and worldwide fame, still wondered: Am I good enough? Am I pretty enough? Will they like me?"* I have to tell you that after hearing Actor Kevin Costner speak these words at Whitney Houston's funeral in 2012, I really realized that this "not enough-ness" was not just isolated to me and those I'd had this conversation with. This struggle also belonged to someone who was world renowned and greatly admired.

Sister, we've all tried to satisfy this void with external things like dating, educational achievements, sex, successful jobs/careers, alcohol, marriage, drugs, hobbies, attending and/or working in the church, charity work, volunteering, food, civic organization involvement, molding the "best" children, purchasing luxury items like expensive cars and the "best" homes, etc. But still...the void, the emptiness.

Sister, YOU Matter!

Well, Sister, I have something I want to share with you...the filling of the void, the completeness you've been searching for *is* attainable. It's within your reach. Guess what? You already have it. It's been inside of you all along. You were born with it. Did you know that? Yep, it's been there since you came to the Earth. It's what I refer to as your Crown, hence the title of the book: *I Am the Crown.* Sister, if you only knew what I know about you. If you only knew how important you are, how valuable you are, your worth. Sister, if you only knew...Sister, YOU Matter!

Sister, say it with me: *"I Am the Crown."* One more time, loudly this time: *"I Am the Crown!"*

Now, Sister, by saying "I Am the Crown," I am not encouraging arrogance, self-centeredness or conceitedness. Sister, I'm encouraging us (women) to stop compromising ourselves for the next man, the next promotion, the next external thing that we think will complete or satisfy us. We compromise ourselves when we engage in activities that are degrading, demeaning, manipulative, and so below our moral and ethical standards. These activities not only harm others but, more importantly, they harm us. They harm our self-esteem, self-identity, our integrity, our self-concept, our image, even our self-worth.

I am so grieved when I see (or hear reports of) my sisters—any woman being—committing crimes, engaging in deviant and degrading acts, and/or sacrificing their families (including their children) for the sake of the next thing that they think will complete them. The situations we allow ourselves to get involved in, the people we become involved with...simply because we do not know our self-worth.

This is not about religion. It's not about race. It is not about culture. It's not about educational achievements. It's not about comparing yourself to the next person. It's not about the next man, the next degree, the next car, the next job, the next...If those next things never occur, you are *still* the Crown. You are still worthy of honor and respect. This is about discovering your self-worth as a woman and unleashing your influence, your power, and your authority in positive and productive ways.

Sister, say it again: "*I Am the Crown*." One more time, "*I Am the Crown*."

Sister, my desire is that as you read this book, you'll really begin to embrace your authority, exercise your influence, evaluate your significance and elevate your worth in and to this world. You are absolutely necessary and a very essential element on this Earth. Yes, an essential element like air, fire, and water—(think back to Science class)—the elements that the Earth cannot exist without. Without you, there would be a huge void. Without you, to somebody, the world would not spin.

You are an essential part of someone's life—someone else's past, present, and/or future, is or will be because of you. Because of you, they are (or will be) who they are. Without you, others cannot fulfill their own purposes. Sister, I want you to rediscover your power/authority, take back your influence. I want you to choose you. I want you to understand how important and essential you are to this world, to this great plan for the world. Without you, the world would be missing something really big; something really great! Something really, YOU!

**Sister, YOU Matter!**

# CHAPTER 1

"You are the only person on earth who can use your ability."

**Zig Ziglar**

1

# CROWN CONFIRMATION

## You Matter

My Dear Sister, my desire is that as you read this book, you will really have a new understanding, a confirmation, of just how important you are to your family, your friends, your community, and most importantly, you'll know how important you are to you.

Sister, YOU Matter! I can't say this enough to you. Some of us are giving up way too early when we were designed to endure. Some of us are settling for mediocre when we're destined for magnificent. Some of us are settling for employee when we were shaped to be an entrepreneur, the employer. Some of us are just surviving when we are destined to strive. We have to reclaim our position, our influence and our authority. We have to realize who we are under all of the clutter we've accumulated over time. It's obscured our view and squelched our drive to pursue something greater. We have to rediscover ourselves, we have to begin speaking and believing, "I Am the Crown."

My heart aches every time I hear of a woman being taking her own life or compromising herself in a degrading, derogatory manner. I immediately ask myself, "Why didn't she know just how much she matters?" I begin to think about all of the women I come into contact with every day–some I know, some I don't. Some I pay attention to, some I don't. But the question is the same: "Does she really know how important she is? "In other words, "Does she know that she matters?"

Every woman being matters! Every girl, pre-teen, teen, young adult, middle adult, and seasoned adult woman being matters. Sister, YOU Matter!

Regardless of your color, culture, or creed–Sister, YOU Matter!

Regardless of your socio-economic, sexual, or social status–Sister, YOU Matter!

Regardless of your friend status, your likes, your comments–Sister, YOU Matter!

Regardless of your sexual preference–straight, lesbian, transgender, or unsure–Sister, YOU Matter!

Regardless of your age, your physical, emotional, and/or mental health challenges–Sister, YOU Matter!

Regardless of your job title or your employment status–Sister, YOU Matter!

Regardless of your fears, weaknesses, imperfections–Sister, YOU Matter!

Regardless of your past or your future–Sister, YOU Matter!

Regardless of your failures, incompleteness, disappointments–Sister, YOU Matter!
Regardless of your strengths, accomplishments, successes–Sister, YOU Matter!
I'm so tired of losing my sisters to mental and physical prisons, to homicides and suicides because we don't know we matter. I'm tired of us–women beings–selling and/or butchering our bodies, sacrificing our

souls, deceiving our minds and closing off our hearts simply because we don't know we matter. That current situation that seems so difficult, it's just that way for right now. Tomorrow, or even the next minute, can be totally different. Sister, YOU Matter! Say it again, "I Am the Crown!!"

## What's in the "Matter?"

You are.

You are crucial to the well-being of this Earth. There is a very specific purpose for you. The purpose was designed even before you were created. "Matter," in the scientific sense, explains the essence of everything around us. Matter, in the sense of *I Am the Crown*, applies to you–everything about you.  Every success, every failure, every disappointment, every accomplishment, every win, every loss...every *everything* matters because it created you and shaped you. And guess what? Sister, YOU Matter!

Let's examine the word "matter." Scientists say that matter is everything around you. Matter makes up everything you can see (like food and clothes) and some things you cannot see (like smells). Matter is made up of particles so tiny they can only be seen by the most powerful microscope.(Infoplease.com)

This is the same with you, Sister. You matter. Everything about you matters. All of the quirks, qualms, differences, choices–all of these attributes make you, and dear Sister, all of it matters because you matter. Think of your experiences, preferences, differences as the tiny particles that help to make you uniquely you. You are uniquely designed to be just who you are at this time in your life. You are exactly where you need to be at this time in your life. There may be some areas in your life that you want or need to change, but even in those areas, you matter. Just like the atoms are needed to make up matter, EVERY aspect of your life was and is needed to develop you.

**But I'm Different**

Yes, you are. And guess what? So is every other person on this planet. It was designed that way from the beginning of time. No one person is exactly like any other person on Earth. We were made that way. Even children born as multiples have their own personalities and preferences, although they may look exactly alike.

Wouldn't it be awesome if we could learn to celebrate our uniqueness and the uniqueness of others? I think that if we begin to do this, it will put everybody on an equal playing field and lessen some of the tension and extremes.

👑 What's weird about you?

_____

_____

👑 What makes you different from others?

_____

_____

**Why Do I Matter?**

There is a great plan for you: a plan for your success, a prosperous plan, a plan for your good. This plan was designed long before you were even conceived; long before you were ever even thought of. You are not a mistake, regardless of the circumstances of your conception. You were meant to be on this Earth. The simple act of having sex does not guarantee pregnancy, nor does pregnancy always guarantee birth. It's all about timing. It's all about the great plan for your life.

So, for the person reading this book who's been told (or who thought) they were a mistake, you were not, you are not. You are essential to a great plan for this world. Did you know that you–and only you–were created to achieve a very specific task in your lifetime? No one else can do the job. It's your duty and only your duty. No one else can complete it and the world will miss something really big if you don't complete your assignment. Sister, YOU Matter!

Sister, think about it...

We are the voice of reason.
We are the heart of the home.
We are the thermostat in the room.
We are the décor in the building.
We are the details of the big picture.


We, the woman beings, were created to carry life. Physically only the female of most species (I understand the seahorse is different) can naturally carry a growing being. Our bodies were even designed to produce a complete nutrition that can be given to our infant children. Everything about our being, our essence, is about giving and nurturing life. Without you–the woman being–there would be no natural carrier of life. Not only do we carry physical bodies within our bodies, we also carry the emotional and spiritual aspects of life within our hearts.

We are the seat of emotions. Most times, we are the touchy-feely piece of human relationships. We bring the compassion, sympathy, and empathy to most situations. We have the innate ability for details. Most of us naturally plan and execute the necessary, intricately detailed steps to complete projects and tasks. We are able to do this so well because we consider feelings and circumstances and try our best to incorporate them into the big global plans.

In most cases, we make the house a home. We decorate. We accentuate. We beautify. We add the "soft" touch to the wood; the hard, rough, and cold brick, the slabs of concrete. Regardless of the house's dimensions, it's usually the feel of the inside of the house that sells it...realtors call it "staging." Sister, YOU Matter!

Sister, I often wonder how different our world would be if only we, the women beings, knew that we mattered, and just how much we really matter. I really do believe that if we knew just how much we mattered that our men and children would value women in a way that could return the world to its sweetness, its innocence–its sincere appreciation for the woman being and for mankind and life as a whole.

## The Creation

To really help you understand our importance in this world, let's go the beginning: The Creation.  Sister, did you know that only *after* woman was created, that the Creation was called "perfect?" (Some versions say "very good" [Genesis1:31.]) Prior to that, "and it was good" described the creation. Now, I'm not saying that there's anything wrong with "good," but I feel awfully special with the "very good" or "perfect" description after the woman was included. I hope this helps us understand how important we women are to the big picture.  If that's not enough, did you realize that in the Garden of Eden, the serpent approached the woman, not the man? Even the serpent knew how important we were/are to God's plan. He knew the magnitude of the woman's influence in our homes, families, with our friends, and in our community. Sister, YOU Matter!

## Beyond the Creation

Now, let's examine our importance from a worldly historical perspective. Do you know the number of wars that have been fought for you? The number of struggles endured for you? The number of lives lost for you? Do you realize that the historic revolutionary events of this world were mostly based on the belief that all people (yes, even the woman) should be treated humanely, with dignity, and with respect? Remember hearing and/or reading about the Civil War, the Women's

Suffrage Movement, the Civil Rights Movement, the Equal Pay for Equal Work Movement, the global United to End Genocide Movement, the Movement to End Female Genital Mutilation? The listing could go on and on and on. There are still so many struggles all over the world for just our basic rights.

## Sister, YOU Matter!

Sister, I want you to know how valued you are in this great plan for our world. You are absolutely essential. The world can't go on without you; therefore, speak it again: "I AM THE CROWN."

## The Crown

Why the Crown? What's so significant about the Crown?

Remember when we were young girls? Most of us thought being a princess would be the best position ever. We imagined that as a princess we could have whatever we wanted, say whatever we wanted and do whatever we wanted. Some of us even owned a crown or tiara, a magic wand, and even the "glass slippers" to wear during those crowing moments of play. We felt so important and confident. We were all smiles and giggles and everyone knew to give us the royal treatment because we were the princess—we were wearing the crown. And guess what? We expected the royal treatment, too. So it's with that image and all the pomp and circumstance that we began to proclaim our importance again. Only this time, we're going to say, "I Am the Crown."

Remember those times when there would be that one person in the play group who didn't know the rules about how to treat the person wearing the crown? The rest of the play group quickly "trained" him or her. It's this same type of confidence I'm describing when I use the words "influence" and "authority" throughout the book in relation to *being* the Crown. Visualize wearing that crown on your head and holding that wand in your hand. You know that if you just touch something with that wand, something will change simply because you are wearing the crown, and only those with influence and authority get to wear the crown.

Crowns have been around for a long time but have not lost their symbol of importance or prominence. Crowns come in all shapes, sizes, and colors (just like us). Some come with jewels, some without (some of us like 'bling' and some don't). Crowns usually indicate that the person wearing it is important, powerful, has influence, and is worthy of respect, honor, and glory. The crown itself, not so much the person wearing it, usually draws the attention.

Also, a crown represents a specific status. Most times, when we see a crown on a person's head, we assume that he or she is regal and important, just by the mere fact that they are wearing a crown. When we see a person wearing a crown, we immediately begin to ask questions like: "Who's that?" "What's their title?" "Where are they from?" We even begin to act differently just because we are in the presence of a person wearing a crown.

Additionally, the wearing of the crown warrants expectations. Usually we have some expectations for the person wearing the crown like what he should wear, how she should behave in public and private, how he should treat his family and his friends, etc. We also expect that they are entitled to 'royal' treatment from others.

Crowns have been worn since ancient times to symbolize the importance of the wearer. They represent power, authority, status, honor and victory. Sometimes they are decorated with jewels and sometimes they can be as simple as a cap or turban worn on the head. Here are some interesting facts I found about the history of the crown:

- "The crown, in the ancient world, came in many shapes and forms. They were made of very costly material, symbolizing royalty and sovereignty. The crown was an emblem of power and legitimacy and a symbol of transcendent authority upon monarchs and rulers throughout history. The crown is a valued and ornamented headgear worn by rulers especially when appearing in public or in their official role as king or queen. Ancient heads of state surrounded themselves with the optics of glory beginning with the coronation ceremony when they were crowned and seated upon a throne indicating their authority, power and importance to the audience they ruled and intimidated into submission."(Bible-history.com)

- "The important piece of regalia, it [the crown] is a potent symbol bestowing virtues or power, righteousness, legitimacy and glory on the wearer." (swide.com)

- "…from the earliest times, a distinctive head ornament that has served as a reward of prowess and a sign of honor and dominion."(Britannica.com)

Now that we know more about the crown's history, let's shift the focus back to you–the internal you–the part that I refer to as the "Crown." It's your essence, your being, your character. It's all those elements that make you you. It's your uniqueness. It's your distinction, your individuality, your exclusivity, your "You." It's what's at the core of your being. It's the "jewels" you know you have but you're waiting on someone else to see them; to give them value; to validate them for you.

Does this type of self-talk sound familiar to you? "I know I'm a good person; why doesn't he/she recognize it?" "I know I can do a good job; why don't they choose me?" If so, here's your reminder: the completeness that you are seeking is already in you. You already possess it. Sister, I want you to understand that you are the Crown. You are the Crown. You are worthy of honor. You are important. You are precious. You are valuable. You are powerful. You matter. Sister, you are a woman, a wonderful being so absolutely essential to this world's existence. You deserve respect, honor and glory–all of the adoration expected and given to a Crown. Sister, you are the Crown. The Crown is who you are here on Earth. It's your self-worth. Sister, YOU Matter!

**Who Am I?**

"If you don't distinguish yourself from the crowd,
you'll just be the crowd."

*Rebecca Mark*

This is a very common question that we ask ourselves during different phases of our lives but I'm not sure if we ever really answer it truthfully. We've become so accustomed to doing, being busy, tackling the next accomplishment, and acquiring titles and/or things that we commonly respond to this question by listing our life roles and/or our titles. For instance: I am a sister, a mother, a daughter, an administrator, a writer, etc.

Okay, what are your roles/titles? List them below.

_____  _____  _____

_____  _____  _____

_____  _____  _____

Now that you have listed your roles/titles, the question still remains: "Who am I?" Who are you really? Underneath all of the titles we may carry, who are we deep-down? This may be a difficult question to ask yourself, but it is an important one for you to answer because you are not a label, you're a person.

For so long, I chose to allow my life roles to define me. I would be utterly crushed when I didn't get the promotion, accepted to the college, or selected for a position or approached for a date. As a matter of fact, because I believed that my life roles defined me, I was all too eager to continuously accept new roles even when I did not have the time to honor all of the commitments I had made or was making. I encourage you to no longer allow your roles in life to define who you are. I have learned that this type of lifestyle is stressful, tiring, and it kept me stuck on needing something external to fill the emptiness.

Most times, our roles in life change.  Sister, change is a very natural element of life. But because so much of our identity is intertwined with our roles, the life role changes really adversely affect us. The changes often cause frustration, anger, and sometimes even depression–not so much because of the change but because of what the roles/titles mean to us.

Let's explore some common life roles/titles of women to better illustrate my point.

<u>Student</u>

I think we are forever students in this school of life. There is always an opportunity to learn something new if we are open to it.

All of us can relate to the formal student experience: elementary, middle school, junior high, and high school. Some of us can even relate to higher education experiences. These mandated student experiences made up the early educational years in our lives, when the student title was our "spot" in life. The late nights, the pop quizzes, the tests, the exams, the stress, the high expectations of others. For most of us, we strived to earn the highest grade possible in each course. But then comes the failing grade, the failing score. It's not what others expected of us, and it's definitely not what we expected of ourselves. These particular failing grades could mean the difference between graduating on time or not. Does the student title still define you?

<u>Employee</u>

It's the accomplishment you've waited on a long time. You finally have stable employment. It's not your ideal job, but it'll work for right now; it's a job you can at least be proud of. You come in early, work late, and even take work home. Your work product is impeccable, flawless—because that's just the way you do things—you strive for excellence.

You apply for the promotion, knowing that you have "earned" it because of all of your hard work and extra effort. But somehow the promotion does not come, although you're more than qualified. Or even worse, your current job is phased out or you're fired and you are no longer employed. Suddenly your job is gone. You search to find another one in your field and you're told that you are either overqualified or under qualified. You are devastated. You are embarrassed. You struggle with what to say to others when asked about where you work or what you do.

If the need for the job was only tied to income, you'd be okay with any job that paid a decent salary but this job was more than that. This job meant so much to you. It was finally a job that could define you; it was a huge achievement to have finally been given this particular title/position. This job was finally a step in the right direction regarding your career. There's the emptiness again, the void. Does the role of employee still define you?

Wife

When you said yes to the proposal and married him, you knew this would be the fulfillment you needed, the satisfaction for which you yearned. You even settled on some of the 'items on your list' because he was a good guy and, hey, no one's perfect.

Now, you're single…divorced, widowed or even abandoned. How do you move forward? You had ensured that you were a good wife. You put up with so much and endured so much but still, you're single again. What is there to live for? Your spouse is no longer with you. Your friends were friends with you both. There's the emptiness again, the void. A loss is a loss. Even if the marriage is the worst of situations imaginable, it's still a loss and it's the type of loss that makes us question who we really are. It makes us question our worth, our value. Does the role of wife still define you?

Mother

You've been a good mother to your children. You have sacrificed so much. I mean, you've been there for everything:  the sports, the homework, the recitals, the doctors' appointments, the field trips, the staying up all night long, the dances, the prom, the graduation…and even the "not so proud moments" like the principal's office, the youth detention center, etc. You've done for them when you couldn't do for yourself. Finally, your goal, what you've worked so hard to achieve–that child taking care of themselves–happens. The child moves out of the home for college, the military, or just to start life on their own. This was the last child living at home; no other children are home now. You don't know what to do with your time, your money, or your energy. You may even begin to feel useless and unloved because the children no longer need you to the extent they once did. At this stage of life, it's commonly referred to as the "empty nest syndrome." There's the emptiness again, the void. Does the role of mother sill define you?

> "You may find the worst enemy or best friend in yourself."
>
> **English Proverb**

Sister, you are not defined by your success in school, your job, your marital status or your children. Being single, dating, or married is not *who* you are. Being single does not make you less valuable than the woman who's not. You are not a baby mama. You are not your education level. You are not an easy lay. You are not a trick. You are not a CEO. You are not an evangelist. You are not your earned degree. You are not an addict. You are not a prostitute. You are a human being. You are a woman. You were wonderfully created. You were marvelously made. Remember, you were–and still are–the Crowning glory to the creation. You were the icing on the cake. You made the creation perfect. Sister, YOU Matter!

Please write this statement in the space provided below and speak it to yourself as you write it.

I am a human being.

I am a woman.

I am wonderfully created.

I am marvelously made.

I matter!

_____

_____

_____

_____

_____

_____

Here's your confirmation:

I AM the Crown!!! Say it loudly: I AM the Crown!!!

*Sister, YOU Matter!*

# CHAPTER 2

"Don't choose the one who is beautiful to the world; choose the one who makes your world beautiful."

*Author Unknown*

2

# CROWN COMPONENTS

Now that we are beginning to understand who we are and that we (women) are the Crown, let's be creative for a little bit. Let's actually make a design for our Crown. This chapter will be a deviation from the rest of the book. This chapter is intended to help you paint that visual picture of your internal Crown. At the completion of this chapter, you will have a picture of a beautiful physical Crown to remind you of your awesomely beautiful and unique internal Crown. This chapter is simple and fun.

In order to create, to make something, the most efficient way is to make a plan, a written design for what we want. It's just like building a house (or any building for that matter). There has to be a design, a blueprint, so that the builders know what materials are needed and the dimensions of what's to be created.

The plan is needed so that the appropriate resources can be allocated to the project. Resources like people, materials and money. So for our Crown planning, we need to consider the materials that will be used to make our Crowns.

**My Foundation**

What will be your Crown's foundation/base material? The foundation of the Crown will be the support to all of the other adornments of the Crown. We commonly see physical Crowns that are gold or silver. We

18

also see children's Crowns made of paper or plastic.

So, what's the role of the foundation? Why is it so important? We often hear that "a good foundation is crucial to success," but why? Here are two common definitions for foundation: 1. *an underlying basis or principle for something*; and 2. *the lowest load-bearing part of a building, typically below ground level. (Oxforddictionaries.com)*

Do you notice any similarities with these two definitions? They both communicate a soundness, a concreteness, a steadiness. The foundation of anything is its base, its footing. It's the starting point/the beginning, the base/bottom. It's what's at the core, the heart of a thing. It's its essence, fundamentals, principles. Did you know that the most essential component of any object, building or system is its infrastructure? If the foundation is unsteady and cannot support the structure that is resting on it, then how stable is the structure?

What will you choose for your Crown's foundation?


## My Gems/Jewels

Will your Crown be adorned with gems—you know, the pretty jewels we women-beings, typically love so much? What are the colors and/or names of the gems? Although the gems of a Crown may be considered optional, in all honesty, they are what makes each Crown unique. They will distinguish your Crown from the next person's Crown. You see, as women, we are all Crowns, but we are very unique. We lose our effectiveness when we try to be like someone else. Generally, a Crown is custom made for the person wearing it. The Crown's gems/jewels are uniquely arranged and include multiple shapes (cuts) and sizes. There are also a variety of colors. All of these characteristics only further enhance the Crown's beauty, uniqueness and radiance.

Which gems/ jewels will your Crown have?

What will be standard of your Crown's jewels—authenticity, rarity, purity, strength, clarity?

Will they be large, small or a combination of sizes?

Draw a picture of your Crown. The next page has intentionally been left blank for your use. Take your time and make a beautiful picture. Remember, this is your vision for what your internal Crown looks like.

Choose one foundation material.

Choose nine jewel/gem types or colors you would like to see on your Crown.

I promise, these specifics will make sense later.  I pinkie swear!

# YOUR CROWN PICTURE

*Sister, YOU Matter!*

# CHAPTER 3

"Creation is only the projection into form of that which already exists."

*Bhagavad Gita*

3

# CROWN CREATION

## What Do I Already Have?

Now that you have a visual of your beautiful internal Crown, we have to create it. We have to take all of the selected materials and assemble the Crown you've designed. Now, this is going to take some work and depending on which type of foundation materials and gems you selected, it could be a long hard process. Some aspects of your Crown will be more difficult than others to put in place.

Using the construction scenario again, let's identify our starting point. Where will the designed structure be built? What type of land is it? What needs to be done to the land to get the site ready for construction? For instance, is it hilly? It is flat? Will the ground be ideal for supporting a structure like the one designed? These are common questions that have to be answered prior to beginning the actual building of the structure.

It's the same for assembling our Crown. What's already there? Is what's already there suitable for the Crown you've designed? How can what you already have be incorporated into your Crown design? You know there's much value in what you already possess. It's those hidden treasures. They can be repurposed, cleaned up–and add "umph" to your Crown. For the purpose of our Crown's assembly, we will explore some of our current habits, thoughts and actions that are not needed to be the woman you were created to be.

## Imposter Traits

The "not needed" current habits, thoughts, and actions would be equivalent to thorns, dirt, thistles, precious metal coloring (not the actual metal) and knock-off gems in our materials selected for our Crowns. We would not choose these for our Crowns and would not take a person seriously who wore a Crown made of or with these materials. Well, we have accumulated some imposter character traits–they look like the real thing, but aren't–that were never intended for us and will not enhance the beauty of our Crown. Some examples (these are a few but there are many others) of imposter traits that we've unintentionally accumulated:

| | | | |
|---|---|---|---|
| Bitterness | Shame | Worry | Envy |
| Guilt | Critical of Others | Self-pity | Condemnation |
| Unresolved Anger | Lust | Desperation | Self-doubt |
| Selfishness | Inability to Forgive | Greed | Critical of Self |
| Fear | Busyness | Ungrateful | Pride |

Identify which of these imposter traits you've carried, or are carrying, in your life. Rank them in descending order regarding their prevalence in your life beginning with #1, which will represent the most prevalent. Try to identify at least ten traits. There may be others not listed here that you may want to list. *(Hint: You will need all ten later in the book.)*

1.                              6.

2.                              7.

3.                              8.

4.                              9.

5.                              10.

The imposter traits you have identified have served some sort of purpose in your life. We, human beings, generally nurture these not-so-pleasant traits to cope with the not-so- pleasant experiences in life. For instance, when we lose someone who is special to us, we may unintentionally choose any one of the traits listed to "protect" us from feeling the pain the next time (if there is a next time). Unfortunately, because we've chosen these adverse methods to deal with the unpleasant experience, we increase our chances of having a similar experience again and again and again. So, over time if we are not careful, the disappointment becomes fear; fear becomes anger; unresolved anger becomes bitterness; and bitterness becomes hatred, either towards others or ourselves. (*Hint: Hurting people hurt people. We'll talk more about this in Chapter 6.*)

Grief

I want to take some time now and talk about grief. Grief can help or hinder us as we develop our Crowns and recognize the vastness of our influence. Dealing with it in a healthy way will help us.  An unhealthy resolution, or no resolution at all, will definitely cripple our internal Crown's development and radiance. Unresolved grief can become depression, bitterness, anger, and/or self-hatred. Unresolved grief will sabotage your wonderful life plan, your future, and snuff out the glow of your inner beauty.

Did you know that grieving is a healthy response to any loss? Did you know that grieving is also a process? Many times we want to just get over the pain associated with the loss we've experienced. However, there is no predetermined allowed amount of time to deal with grief. Still, it has to be dealt with appropriately. It won't just magically go away because we choose not to go through it or choose not to feel it.

Grieving is a very natural response to losing something or someone that's special to us. When the word 'grieve' is used, we generally think about the death of someone special to us but grieving should not be isolated to only the human death experience. Some of us have lost things via natural disasters, theft, deception or financial decline (i.e., foreclosures, repossessions, etc.) Some of us have lost people due to death, separation, divorce, physical moves, or relationship maturity. Some of us are even grieving over living but physically and/or emotionally absent parents, guardians and/or spouses. For example, although the parent/guardian, is living (or was living during our childhood,) it was a loss to us because the parent/guardian was not available physically and/or emotionally. This same concept can also be applied to spouses as well. We may be physically in the same house with each other but emotionally we are planets apart.

Sister, if you haven't grieved your losses in your life, I encourage you to do so. You will remain in an unhealthy and counterproductive space if you don't. You may have to seek professional assistance with this grieving process and it's okay to do so. Sometimes we need help getting to a healthier state. It is just like becoming physically fit. Some of us can "just do it" and get the desired results seemingly instantly. Others of us, like me, need the expertise of a professional fitness trainer to guide us through the process. The professionals know what we need, how to teach us, and even how to motivate us to do it.

To give you more information regarding the grieving process, I have listed below some common stages of grief:

- Denial
- Guilt/Pain
- Anger/Bargaining
- Reflection/Loneliness (Depression)
- Working Through
- Acceptance/Hope

This listing is not all inclusive and there are several popular theories that are used when explaining the grieving process. The stages of grieving can happen at any time and in any order during the grieving process, and some stages may be repeated. However, denial is generally the beginning step and acceptance is usually the final one.

Below are some common signs and symptoms of grief from Griefwatch.com:

| **Physical** | **Emotional** | **Social** | **Behavioral** |
| --- | --- | --- | --- |
| Change in appetite | Numbness | Dependent | Forgetfulness |
| Fatigue | Anger | Avoiding others | Searching for the deceased |
| Sleeping problems | Relief | Lack of interest | Slowed thinking |
| Hyperactive or under active | Guilt | Overly sensitive | Needing to retell the story of the loved one's death |
| Crying and sighing | Anxiety | Lack of initiative | Dreams of the deceased |
| Feelings of emptiness | Abandonment | Withdrawn | Wandering aimlessly |

## Anger

Additionally, there is one specific step of the grieving process that I want to pay special attention to: anger. Some of us are angry and have been for so long that we don't even realize we're angry. We've been told that anger is something that we should not feel; that it is unhealthy to feel anger. This is not true. Anger is a very natural emotion. It's an indicator that something is wrong.

Anger should prompt us to change something, even if it's our perception of a person, place, or event. It is how we choose to respond to anger that is positive or negative—not the anger itself. If we respond positively, the anger is helpful to us and those around us.

However, if we respond negatively to anger, it will be hurtful to (and possibly destroy) us and those around us. We can easily label people as angry when they physically act out or are abusive to themselves, to others, or toward property. Maybe you have noticed that anger management courses have become very popular over the last few years. These courses are designed to help the "perpetrator" (the doer of the violent acts) learn more positive ways to "manage," or respond to, their anger. But I want to spend some time on some of those not-so-obvious negative ways that we, girls and women, tend to express our anger.

### Just "Girls Being Girls"

Maybe you've heard the saying "Just girls being girls." It seems to be a common response to describe teenage girls behaving badly. It's a phrase we tend to hear during those junior high/middle school years. You know, the taunting, badgering, saying mean and degrading things to or about others, the throat-cutting gossip, even lying about others to intentionally make them look bad to their peers. Generally, the "perpetrators" are a small group of girls who have managed to lure others into being their allies, "friends," until the truth about their motives is revealed.

When the layers of the "mess" are pulled back, generally it centers on a boy. The girl liked a boy who didn't like her and she's angry because of it. Either the boy liked some other girl, just did not like the girl, or he may not have even known that the girl liked him. So the malicious attacks on the boy, his friends, and other girls who may like the boy—even only as a platonic friend—begin. These attacks can become very vicious. It hurts so many other people; and in the end, the girl is still angry and she still does not gain the boy.

Ladies, I have a secret: If the boy or man likes you, he'll come to you. You don't have to fight for him or create a big mess about it!

*Just girls being girls*? No, this is just girls being mean. It's this meanness (unresolved anger) that we take into adulthood. Here's what it may look like in the adult world: We attempt to sabotage the success of our co-workers (lying to or about them, not assisting them even when they have asked for our help, gossiping, creating division among co-workers). We can't trust anybody because we expect them to treat us the way we treat others; we can't support or congratulate our Sister on her new promotion, marriage, baby, business, home, or car because we are still angry about some unresolved issue, and/or are upset because we don't have what we think we want or "deserve".

Have you noticed the increase in the videos that we are posting online that show us staging fights with other Sisters? There are usually other women in the video cheering the "perpetrator" on, encouraging the next "cuss" word or verbal and/or physical assault. This victim is usually so unsuspecting and caught off guard by the perpetrator's actions. But it becomes increasingly obvious that the attack was planned and the perpetrator intends to harm the unsuspecting victim. The posting of the video on social media is to add insult to the victim's injury.

Sister, this is not just girls being girls, this is girls being mean and women behaving badly. It's not cute and it certainly does not look good or speak well of our Crown. It speaks volumes regarding the lack of value we have for our own self-worth.

**What Do I Need?**

Now, how do we take what we currently have, these imposter traits that we've identified, and use them in the development of our desired Crown? To get your Crown ready, some refining has to take place. This will be hard work but well worth the process. I promise.

Did you know that a beautiful diamond, commonly referred to as a "girl's best friend," was once a lump of coal before the refining process was applied? In essence, "a refining process separates everything into useful substances."(Science.howstuffworks.com)

Here is a definition of "refining" from www.dictionary.reference.com that I like: *to purify from what is coarse, vulgar or debasing; make elegant or cultured; to become more fine, elegant or polished; to improve, inserting finer distinction, superior elements, etc.*

Another "refining" process is pruning. Pastor Joel Osteen once said: "Pruning is putting me in a position to blossom. Pruning season always positions us for new growth. Pruning always leads to blooming."

Dictionary.com lists the following regarding pruning: "to cut or lop off (twigs, branches, or roots); to cut or lop superfluous or undesired twigs, branches, or roots from; trim; to rid or clear of (anything superfluous or undesirable); to remove (anything considered superfluous or undesirable)."

See, pruning is not a haphazard cutting of the plant. Instead, it serves a valuable purpose for the plant: preservation. It's the removal of what's no longer needed to maintain the plant's healthy growth.

Well, we've got some work to do. Those imposter traits like anger, jealousy, grief, guilt, etc. have to be pruned to yield a more productive and healthy you—the Crown. We want to replace them with what I call "purpose traits."

<u>Purpose Traits</u>

Purpose traits will be the foundation and gems in our Crowns. These traits will add the glow and radiance to our Crowns. They will promote a healthy regeneration of some of those "dead" areas of our lives. You know, sometimes if we remove the seemingly dead part of a plant, new growth emerges from the plant. Have you noticed that in our young years, when we cut our hair, it grows faster? It's almost like freeing up space for what's been waiting to sprout and grow but couldn't because the space was already occupied with unproductive, old or dead stuff.

For the purpose of developing our Crowns, we are going to mature—allow to blossom—some traits and characteristics that are already in us. I affectionately call them our purpose traits, the foundation and jewels in our Crowns...

| Love | Joy | Peace | Patience |
|------|-----|-------|----------|
| Kindness | Goodness | Faithfulness | |
| Gentleness | Self-Discipline | Contentment | |

| Purpose Trait | Explanation |
|---------------|-------------|
| Love | **Affection for others. Great and warm affection. Unselfish, loyal, and benevolent concern for the good of another.** |
| | Love colors every facet of our life. It is the basis for everything we do, say and think in our lives. |
| | I think the world would be a better place in which to live if we all, Christian or not, learned to love others like we love ourselves. |

This is why discovering our self-worth is so essential. The more we discover our self-worth (our value), the more we will unselfishly love ourselves. Consequently, the more we love ourselves, the more sincere and unselfish love and genuine concern we can give others.

**Joy**

**Keen pleasure; elation. Success or satisfaction. A feeling of extreme pleasure, happiness, and/or contentedness that comes from a sense of well-being.**

Joy, once realized, is ongoing and is the assurance from within that everything (the good and not so good) in life is just the way it should be. Joy is not dependent on the circumstances, things, or events in our lives.

Joy and happiness are not the same, although often times the words are used interchangeably. Happiness is often temporary and is dependent on good and pleasant things happening in our lives. The 'happiness' feeling is always dependent on the next good thing, happening, or event. Remember, we need stable materials for our Crown, so we need joy instead of happiness.

**Peace**

**Serenity. Freedom from the negative effects of upsetting thoughts or feelings.**

Peace is inside each of us. We yearn for it, especially during rough times in our lives. Inner peace will allow us to smile frequently, even when we don't feel like it. We will be less likely to judge ourselves and others when we experience inner peace. Our tendency to worry will become a last resort, if an option at all.

Inner peace will allow us to just let life happen – to go with the flow –in lieu of always forcing everything to go the way we think it should. It will allow us to just enjoy the moment, each moment, for what it is at that time. Inner peace will ignite us to just simply enjoy and appreciate life in any situation.

**Patience**     **A willingness to stick with things. Long suffering. Putting up with pain or trouble without complaint.**

Patience is definitely a learned trait, and unfortunately, the only way to learn this trait is by living through trials and difficult circumstances. Think about it this way: children are not patient regarding anything. They want what they want...when they want it. This patience trait is definitely learned by trial and error for adults, too. We generally learn, the difficult way, that getting what we want instantly may not be what is best for us or our wonderful life plan that is already developed for us.

**Kindness**     **A sense of compassion in the heart. Easily handled; not wild; Mild.**
*(This trait is a focus on others; the kindness shown to others)*

The best illustration of kindness is what we

see a new mom giving her newborn child. She is so gentle. Her every act is performed with such care, concern and diligence to provide the very best for her child.

Kindness shown to others is also very soothing, especially when exhibited in situations where the exact opposite is expected. For instance, consider when someone is rude to you but you respond with kind words or actions. You may even go out of your way to help that particular person...talk about "killing them with kindness!"

**Goodness**

**Excellence of morals and behavior. The quality or state of being good; Good is defined as suitable for use.**

Synonyms for goodness include integrity, honesty, worth, value and morality. Goodness implies positive character or a standard of right conduct.

**Faithfulness**

**Unwavering. Reliable; an undivided heart.**

Faithfulness is the ability to stay committed in spite of the ups and downs. This trait can be applied to any area of your life.

**Gentleness**

**Not needing to force our way in life. To put up with injury or abuse.**
*(This trait is a focus on self.)*

When I think of gentleness expressed towards ourselves, I think of our ability to be careful with ourselves. Examples include not being harsh on ourselves and giving compassion and mercy to ourselves the way we generously give them to others. Forgiving ourselves and loving ourselves are some beginning and very necessary ongoing steps towards being gentle to ourselves.

**Self-Discipline**

**Able to marshal and direct our energies wisely. Control over one's own impulses, emotions, actions, i.e. your will.**

Self-discipline, sometimes called self-control, can be demonstrated by our ability to not say or do what comes to mind but to choose our words and actions in consideration of others and ourselves.

**Contentment**

**Satisfaction; Ease of mind. Not desperate for more.**

Contentment is the ability to appreciate and be thankful for everything (the good and not so good) in life and accepting that life is just the way it should be. It's the ability to be okay with the extremes of life.

Here's a quote that I think sums up contentment: *"Two things that could measure who we are: The way we manage when we have nothing, and the way we behave when we have everything." **Author Unknown***

Take a few minutes to determine the strength of your purpose traits using the following rating method: prime, preferred or positive. Remember, we already possess these traits. Some of them are more developed (have a stronger presence) than others.

- Positive=good. Those traits that are generally a little less obvious in our lives and need more cultivating than the preferred traits.
- Preferred=better. Those traits that fall between the prime and positive traits.
- Prime=best. This is a superior quality in you. Others may often compliment you regarding this trait.

Additionally, what actions can you list that demonstrate these purpose traits in your life? For instance, how do you demonstrate love in your life? List them here:

| Positive | Preferred | Prime | Action |
|---|---|---|---|
| Good (needs more cultivation) | Better | Best (a definite strength) | |

**Purpose Trait**
Love
Joy
Peace
Patience
Kindness
Goodness
Faithfulness
Gentleness
Self-Discipline
Contentment

## What Will I Gain?

> "When you stop chasing the wrong things you give the right things a chance to catch you."
>
> ***Author Unknown***

Some of us have become so accustomed to wearing the "look alikes", the imposters, that we no longer even appreciate the value of the real diamond. We say "That's way too expensive" and select a "gem" of inferior quality because it's cheaper. We try so hard to be proud of wearing it. But over time, the "inferior" gem loses its luster and begins to reveal to others that it was a cheap replica. Now sometimes, the replica can cost us a lot, but in the end, it's still not the real "gem."

I learned some years ago that a more productive way to combat negative habits was to replace them instead of focusing on getting rid of them. Let me explain what I mean: If we keep focusing on the negative aspects and channeling our energies and efforts towards not repeating the negative habit(s)–the imposter traits–the change can become very demanding, overwhelming, and may even seem impossible. We may become consumed with thinking about not repeating the negative habit, which means we are still focusing on the negative habit. But if we can find a positive behavior or a positive trait to replace the negative one, we shift our focus to doing the positive and are not thinking so much about the negative one.

I have applied this practice to my own life in various areas. For example, I struggle with maintaining a body weight that I'm comfortable with. I have for years. Some of my struggle is my own unhealthy perception of my body's shape. I most times consider myself overweight regardless of my size because it doesn't look like the ideal body image that I mentally compare to my reflection in the mirror. (I admit, I'm still a work in progress with this one.) So because of my struggle, I have tried a plethora of methods to help me not "look" so "fat".

One method has been dieting. Now, I was NEVER successful with dieting because it seemed so restrictive. The foods that I was not allowed to eat were usually the things I craved but only while I was on the diet. I HAD to have them as I progressed through the diet plan. I would walk around with my list of "do not eat" foods (*negative focus*) and I promise you, it seemed as if those foods were screaming my name even when I did not see them in front of me. It was like a "haunting" of some sort.

I realized and accepted that I am an emotional eater and I love to snack, especially when I'm at work or stressed. So what finally worked for me was focusing on the foods that I could eat (*positive focus*) and those became the foods that I kept around me all the time. Instead of chips, I choose a sweet and salty healthy snack mixture. Instead of sweet cake-type snacks, I choose fruit. I have even embraced eating a modified meal plan—not a diet—for five days of the week. I can eat whatever I want for those other two days. It's kind of like my reward for eating better those other five days. You're probably asking: Don't you sabotage and over-indulge on those two days? Initially, yes, but over time my desire for those "weekend" foods decreased.

Two other areas in which I practice this replacement method are self-talk and self-pity.

Self-Talk

Self-talk is awesome when it's used in a positive way. It can encourage, motivate, and empower us to achieve things not humanly possible. I had to learn to shift my self-talk to the positive aspect. For a long time, my self-talk was demeaning and very negative. I constantly told myself what I couldn't do or couldn't have or couldn't achieve. However, I came to realize over time that most of my negative self-talk did not originate with me. It had been talk deposited into me by other people, most of them meaning well when they spoke those "helpful hints" to me. I began to notice a pattern: After each disappointment, this negative self-talk (usually in the voice of the person who first spoke those words into my life) confirmed the disappointment I had just experienced.

For the longest time after a disappointment, I would hear:*"Your life will never be right because your first mistake was the college you chose. "*These words had been spoken to me by someone whose opinion of me I highly regarded. Although the words were meant to help me find some positive direction in my life at that time, I carried them with me and applied them to other disappointments in my life without even realizing how much the words had negatively affected me. As I reflected back over my life, I began to realize that there were multiple "memory" phrases like this one playing out in my life and being repeated over and over and over again.

So, what finally worked for me? I began to speak positively to myself *especially* after a disappointment. For instance, I say phrases like: "What can I learn from this experience?" "This too, will work for my good." "Everything will work out the way it is supposed to."

Now you try. What positive self-talk do you use or will you use? Write them below.

1.

2.

3.

**Sister, YOU Matter!**

## Self-pity

Sister, self-pity is allowed, sometimes it is absolutely necessary; but only temporarily. However, when I find myself having to have partied in my pity a little too long, I try intentionally to do something else, including something nice for someone else. These activities shift the focus away from me to something or someone else.

My actions are usually simple. For instance, I may work in my flower beds or replant some houseplants. It's a win-win: The plants love the extra attention and respond quite well to the extra care, and it makes me feel good to see some good as a result of my efforts.

Another action that I implement in the midst of my partying in my pity, is to call someone to check on them, or I may send a 'I'm thinking of you' handwritten note to someone via mail. The handwritten notes are all about the other person. I don't add my stuff to it-that would continue the self-pity party. The notes are usually well received and so unexpected because people don't hand write notes to others much anymore. I've been told that the handwriting really communicates how special the person is to me because I took the time to actually write a note to them. Believe it or not, I am encouraged by the "thank you" I receive in response to the note. Again, a win-win for me and the other person.

What are some replacement activities you can do when you realize you have partied too long in your pity? Write them below.

1.

2.

3.

"Every single thing that has ever happened in your life is preparing you for a moment that is yet to come."

*Author Unknown*

Crown Time

So to apply this "replacement" method to our Crowns...

The best way to discover your self-worth is to replace the negative imposter traits with positive purpose traits. Now let's give a new purpose to those foundation materials and gems selected for our Crown designed in Chapter 2.

Remember your diagram/blue print for your Crown in Chapter 2? We are going to match your foundation material and gems with the purpose traits. Love will represent your foundation material but the other nine traits can be represented by any gem/color you chose but it's a package deal. All of the purpose traits must be represented on your Crown. Remember, we are talking about discovering your self-worth, the inner you–the Crown.

| Purpose Traits | Foundation/Base Material | Gem/Color |
| --- | --- | --- |
| Love | | |
| Joy | | |
| Peace | | |
| Patience | | |
| Kindness (Others' focus) | | |
| Goodness | | |
| Faithfulness | | |
| Gentleness (Self focus) | | |
| Self-Discipline | | |
| Contentment | | |

*Sister, YOU Matter!*

# CHAPTER 4

"People who cannot invent and reinvent themselves must be content with borrowed postures, secondhand ideas, fitting in instead of standing out."

*Warren Bennis*

# 4

# CROWN CHECK

Crown Check. Testing...1...2...3. We have confirmed that we are the Crown and have given our foundation and gems purpose, now it's time to determine how well it fits. It's time for a Crown check. This Crown check is like the sound check conducted by a sound technician ensuring that all of the assembled components work well together, that all of the wire and hardware connections are producing the desired outcome.

Think of the Crown you've designed. Isn't it beautiful? Aren't you going to look great wearing it? Remember, there is an awesome plan for you and we have discovered that we already possess the foundation material and all of the gems needed. So we have a blueprint—but how well does it fit? Internally, is our foundation stable and sound? Are those gems going to enhance our "outer fit?"

## The Hardware

You know, we (women) spend so much time ensuring that our outer "fit" is together. We spend a lot of money on all the superficial things: Makeup for the face; the extensions, weave, wigs, relaxers, perms, color, etc. for the hair; false eyelashes; lipstick to coordinate with our outer wear or eye wear; nails and nail polish; cleansers for our skin; the plastic body enhancements...and let's not even get started on the clothes, shoes, and handbags. According to a Huffington Post article published a few years ago, women spend over $426 billion a year on just beauty products alone.

We are obsessed with painting this picture of perfection for our outer selves. So much of our self-value is based on our outer appearance. We spend so much time, money and energy on having our images communicate our value to others. Did you know that according to a recent Beauty World News report that "women wear a face full of cosmetics for nearly 13 hours a day and will have just 11 hours free from it?" The report also stated that of the 2000 women polled, 10% said that "the more makeup they have on, the better they feel" and that well over half of the 2000 women studied said "they feel less confident when completely bare-faced."

Sister, there is absolutely nothing wrong with looking nice on the outside. I encourage all of us to take time to properly groom and adorn ourselves, because the outer appearance is usually our first introduction to others. "Your first impression may be your last impression," was a popular saying when I was growing up. However, our lack of inner beauty could cause our first encounter to be our last encounter with others.

People usually remember more about how we made them feel versus how "pretty" we were. It's that inner beauty, your Crown, your self-worth, that being okay with who you are under the makeup, hair, nails, and clothes, that will matter in the end. That's what will leave the lasting impression. Here's something to consider: all of the "outer" stuff can and will fade as we age (even the plastic enhancements will not last forever), and if our self-worth is dependent on these external qualities, what happens when they no longer exist? Who are we without these things? How do we feel about ourselves when the makeup comes off? Does that beautiful Crown fit after all of the external stuff is gone? Does the inner you match the fabricated outer you? Does the Crown fit?

**Sister, YOU Matter!**

**The Wiring**

For most of us, the physical crown we have designed is very beautiful. Some of us probably feel that it's too pretty for us, too good for us. We begin to think about all of our negative attributes and think there is no way those purpose traits can be manifested in us. But Sister, that is not true. You see, you were designed so that all of these "gems" would radiate through you. You already have them in you. So how do we get them to radiate? Commitment and submission.

Commitment

A quick internet definition search on Bing.com for "commitment" yielded the following words: "the state or quality of being dedicated to a cause, activity, etc."

So, what does that mean exactly? What does that look like? Words like dedication, devotion, allegiance, loyalty, faithfulness and fidelity come to mind and help explain the word commitment. With the aid of these words, I hope we have a better idea of what commitment looks like and its meaning.

What are your commitments? Where do your loyalties lie? To what are you faithful? In what areas of your life are you dedicated? How do you know that you are committed? What proof do you have to show your devotion to these areas?

I've heard it said that by examining a person's finances, one can determine what's important to the person. So looking at your spending. To what do your expenses say you are committed? Career? Food? Clothes? School? Gambling? Making money? God? Family? What does your spending say about your priorities? Are you committed to something stable or something fleeting?

Sister, understand that whatever we are committed to should steer us in the direction we are trying to go. Therefore, our commitments should be to stable, solid principles. Being committed to your job is a good thing but what happens when the job no longer exists? A more stable commitment principle concerning your career/work could be to a positive work ethic. Committing yourself to a positive work ethic can remain constant regardless of your actual work or title. It doesn't change. Characteristics of a positive work ethic can include hard work, dependability, diligence, cooperation, productivity, and self-discipline. Characteristics of this nature can definitely help get you to where you are trying to go, not only in your career, but in other areas of your life as well.

What does commitment entail? How do I become committed to something? Well, let's see...

1. **Make a decision.** Commitment starts with deciding that whatever you are committing to is what you want to do. Without that decision, you will not succeed at being committed. Don't rely on others to make the decision for you. This is your decision and yours alone.

2. **Plan the steps.** Identify the steps you will need to take to be committed. Planning is a process. An effective plan should be simple, realistic, measurable and would minimally contain the following steps:
   a. Goal: Establish your target/objective. (You know; what you want.)
   b. Action: Identify what you'll do (the steps you'll take) to reach your goal.
   c. Results: Observe what happens because of your actions.
   d. Follow up: Analyze the results. Were the results positive or negative? Did you get what you wanted? Did you reach your desired goal? Review the results, learn your lessons **AND**
   e. Repeat: Start the planning process over again either with this same goal (if you did not get the results you wanted), a different goal or even another small step towards a larger goal.

For instance, if your goal is to spend within your budget, identify what actions are needed to do this. Establish a budget. Write it down and then determine where you are overspending. Once the overspending area(s) has been identified, look for ways you can decrease your spending in that area. For example, if your budget for lunch per week is $25 and you realize you are spending more than $25 per week, search for ways to stay within your budget. Can you take your lunch some days? When you think about it, you're already buying groceries for the home. So if you take lunch from home, it could decrease the amount you spend on lunch for the week.

3. **Stay focused.** Stick with the decision. Now, because this is new (or renewed) it will be difficult to stay on track, especially when disappointments or setbacks come. Remember the initial decision. You may have to say out loud to yourself, "I am committed to this regardless of how frustrating and disappointing the circumstances may be. I am committed."

Identify five areas where you would like to become committed or *more* committed:

1.

2.

3.

4.

5.

Now, write a plan for one of the five areas identified.

Goal:

Action:

Results:

Follow-up:

Repeat:


## The "S" Word: Submission

Wait, don't close the book! I know this "S" word is frightening but I promise if you continue to read, you'll better understand this "S" word, submission, from a more approachable perspective.

I have to admit that I struggled with this "S" word for a long time. I hated to hear the word mentioned and developed an attitude pretty quickly when I was expected to submit. Submit to who? Submit to what? *I ain't 'bout to submit to nothing!* Oh and it had better not be a man talking about submitting to him. I was ready to fight, then. A next date, much less a next phone call, was not even up for discussion.

But I've got to tell you, I've learned a thing or two about submission and it's not as bad as it seems. Actually, I've come to respect and embrace it and life is so much easier. You see, submission is absolutely essential to provide support for the gems added to your internal Crown's foundation. It will add a continual and appealing flow to the characteristics of your internal Crown.

When you read or even hear the word 'submission,' does it make you cringe, like it once did for me? Do you associate it with direct or indirect experiences of someone being subjected to bondage, mistreatment, and/or abuse? Submission was never intended to promote coercion or abuse. Submission was all about creating order. The human being has taken this simple pleasure of life and created a nightmare that has led to tension and distrust among people of all ages, races, and sexes. *NOTE: For those who are misusing authority by being abusive to those under our authority, be warned: you will receive what you give. When someone chooses to yield to our authority, it is our responsibility to handle them with care.*

### Fight or Flow

I want to explore another way of viewing submission: it's really your choice to fight or flow with life. We, as women, have become so accustomed to "fighting" our way and attempting to control every aspect of our lives. We've coined these behaviors as being "strong" and "assertive."Some of us have gone to the extreme of trying to control even the pleasurable things in life. We can't even allow life to just happen because it's not planned. If something happens that's not planned, we tend to view it as a failure (and for most of us, we own it as "I've failed" or "I'm a failure").

But Sister, life cannot be controlled. Things will happen that we did not plan for. This realization is the foundation for submission. It's a "let life happen" mindset. A popular saying now is "Live, Love, Laugh." We say this and hang all the art on the wall but are we really living, loving, and laughing–especially if the day's events are not planned? If we are attempting to plan or control every aspect of our lives, then no, we are not.

I know this submission talk is contrary to the current popular belief that one must never surrender or submit. The submission I'm talking about is to yourself–realizing that you can choose a different way. Think of submission as a gift, the gift of no longer having to feel like you have to fight for everything, to control everything. This is the freedom to choose a more serene and peaceful path. This is not oppressive or abusive, it's your choice to learn from life while you live, love, laugh, and dance through the good–and not so good–times in life.

## Live, Love, Laugh and Dance

Submission is the ability to embrace the freedom to live, love, laugh and dance. Now, this is not drifting aimlessly through life without a plan but it's the ability to enjoy life as the plan unfolds. It's the ability to appreciate the ups and downs, the good and the bad, the planned and the unplanned. It's learning lessons from the not so good and then using the lessons to make life, you know, "the plan" I keep referring to, better.

Submission...It's gentle. It's quiet. It's serene. It's the smooth, rhythmic pace of a slow dance following our partner's lead. It's the assurance that, even if life leads us to the end of a cliff, there will be a cliff hanger or a safe place to land already waiting on us. It's the relinquishing of our clenched fists and scowled face. It's a peaceful and tranquil movement that defies our need to control every aspect of life. Sister, this is submission: yielding our choice to another. Submission...it's that gentle dance with life.

Submission is choosing to dance in the rain although the events of your planned day were heavily dependent on the brilliant sunshine. So the divorce happened? Or maybe you've been diagnosed with a chronic illness? No, events like these are generally not planned and, in some cases, they occurred through no fault of your own. But how will you *choose* to respond? Do you fight your way through, blaming others for it? Or do you go with the flow? Do you accept it as an event in life and seek opportunities to grow from it, viewing it as a stepping stone to the next place in your life?

There was a point in my life where I lost most of the important "status" and material things. You know, those things that were supposed to complete me: my job, my marriage, my home, my car, my good professional name and my high credit rating. *These are listed in the order in which I lost them, not so much in the order of importance to me.*

Initially, I felt cheated and robbed because I had worked so hard in my life leading to that point to have all of these attributes, statuses, and things. I have to be very honest here, it was one of the lowest points in my life. I prayed many times that God would not allow me to wake up the next morning. I was embarrassed, ashamed, frustrated, and devastated that my life had somehow spiraled out of control and I'd ended up this way. I walked around for many years labeling myself as a failure because of all I had lost.

I wish I could tell you that I utilized the submission principle. I did not. I fought with everything I had to come out of this slump I found myself in. I remember saying to myself one night while lying in bed," *This will NOT break me. It will make me.* " I made up my mind that night that I would rise from this pit of despair and desolation. I fought for many years. I was fighting every thing, person, place, and situation to get to the next level in regaining all that I had lost. It wasn't until years later that I felt the exhaustion, mentally and physically, of this whole "fight my way back" phase. I remember one day saying to myself, "I'm so tired of feeling like I have to fight for everything".

I realized that I wasn't enjoying life, although I had reestablished myself in many areas of my life. I was so busy fighting my way, making my way and forcing my way through life that I was really missing what life was all about...living. As I began to settle myself, I began to realize that there was already a path established, an easier path. Remember that "life plan" I keep referring to throughout this book? Yeah, that one!

See Sister, there is already a path mapped out for me, a seemingly effortless path just waiting for me to follow. It's like using a GPS for life. When we enter the place we want to go into the navigation system in our vehicles, we generally don't fight the directions given by the device. We just follow the directions; we just flow...It can be the same way with our everyday lives.

Submission...it's your choice. What will you allow to be your authority? Fight or flow?

Identify three life events that were not planned but drastically altered your life plan. Did you fight or flow?

| Event | Reaction: |
| --- | --- |
| | **Fight or Flow** |
| 1. | |
| 2. | |
| 3. | |

How would applying this submission principle to the event, have affected your response? Would your response have been different or the same?

1.

2.

3.

Now, I have to ask: to what are you submitting? If your response is "nothing," you need to rethink your response. We are all submissive to something. Remember, it's about choices. What are you choosing to be the authority in your life?

Whew…we made it through this "S" word information. Sister, I know that this is not what we like to talk about but learning submission is essential to our Crown fitting properly. *Live. Laugh. Love. Dance.*

### *Sister, YOU Matter!*

# CHAPTER 5

"Find out who you are and do it on purpose."

**Dolly Parton**

# 5

# CROWN COORDINATION

Sister, we women wear so many hats. So many life roles are assigned to us. Remember your roles you identified in Chapter 1? Our Crowns should be the same regardless of our role. Your Crown is You. It's your self-worth and your actions in your various roles should reflect just who you are at the core. When we really know who we are and become comfortable (even content) with that person, we will be the same person regardless of the setting. For example, if you are kind, you'll be kind in your home, on your job, and even to a stranger in the community.

WARNING: This chapter may get a little rough. This is the application of all the materials we've discussed to this point. We have drawn the plan and identified what we need to keep and what we don't. Now comes the doing: using what we've designed and understanding how to "work" our Crown in everyday life. The Crown is already made and it looks great but how well we wear it will be paramount in our journey's success.

I think it's equivalent to seeing a suit on the hanger in the store. It's perfect on the hanger. But what really makes us purchase the suit is how well it fits us. We're even willing to purchase it even if a few alterations are needed. And that's what this chapter is about: identifying the Crown alterations that may be needed.

I often wonder how much of our not knowing who we are really affects the world. How does it affect our communities? Our families? We've been given so much authority but I don't think we realize it. We are moving so quickly through life that I think we really can't even begin to comprehend that we already have everything we need to be the women we were created to be.

All of our roles will require use of our Crown's foundation and purpose traits: love, joy, peace, patience, kindness, goodness, faithfulness, gentleness, self-control and contentment. These roles we carry are some of those yet-to-be-discovered treasures in our lives that could really change the world as we know it but first we must know the great potential of our "Crownly" impact.

Crownly Impact

Remember, we are generally the emotional seats (among the sexes) and therefore, we are change agents. Our very presence in the room should change the atmosphere. But most times we walk into a room not knowing who we are or what we encompass and we become like "bulls in the china shop," causing chaos and commotion...or "the big pink elephant in the room," trying to be invisible and unnoticed.

But you are not either of these. You are a woman; you are THE Crown. You carry so many titles and function in so many different roles, coordinating your Crown into all of these aspects of your life is essential. It's essential because it creates balance, exudes strength, endures hardships, and empowers us to be the best we can be regardless of the situations in which we find ourselves.

So how do we wear our Crown and wear it well? We use our foundation and gems (purpose traits) to establish and enhance our lives. We use our Crown to nurture our homes, support our communities, and develop healthy and productive relationships. We have to pay attention to what we illuminate to others; this is a mandate. We wear our Crown well when we take our situations, the good and otherwise, and make the best of them by allowing our Crown to radiate its inner beauty to all we encounter and interact with. This is the application of the Crown.

The Crown is more than just a beautiful adornment, it's a lifestyle. It's you being your internally beautiful you. There are so many areas in our lives, as women, that we have the opportunity to influence the lives of countless others. Our Crowns will leave impressions and legacies for generations to come. Let's explore what the Crown's application may look like as a mother, mentor, wife, dating relationship partner, and neighbor. The **Crown Coordination** sections within this chapter will give application tips that you may want to consider in your daily Crown walk.

**Sister, YOU Matter!**

**Mother**

> "A mother holds her children's hands for a while...
> their hearts forever."
> **Author Unknown**

Mama, Mom, Mommy, Ma —whatever name you go by, it's probably one of the most influential positions in your life. Your Crown radiates in more ways than you may be aware of in this role. This position should not be taken lightly. In no other area in your life will you have the authority to greatly influence the generations to come. I want to spend some time examining how we can transition this often overwhelming parenting responsibility to a guarded and reverenced place of influence.

First, I want to remind you of something: You know our children are a gift to us, right? That's right, planned or unplanned, each and every one of them—yes, they are a gift. Our children are not our property. They do not belong to us. They are not our possessions. They are gifts and just as with any other gift that we receive, we are to be grateful, take good care of them, and exercise good stewardship in our parenting of them. It's really important that we use our Crown wisely in this area of our lives because of the impact that our children will have in the community as they grow and mature. Our impact on them will also directly influence our children's impact on their own children... and their children's children and for generations to come.

Parenting is more than birthing a baby. Parenting is more than providing for the physical and financial needs of the child. Parenting is nurturing the life you've carried and pushed into the world or in some cases, the life given to you by adoption or placement. Parenting is giving your child the emotional and spiritual foundation (in addition to the mandated physical requirements), so they are equipped to live independently (not dependent on you) and productively in the world outside of your home. Whatever we expose our children to in our home will most likely be what they expect and reflect in the world.

<u>Being THE Parent</u>

Are we being THE parent? I ask this question because I have become concerned by the level of disrespect that I see and hear constantly from our children towards adults and/or authority figures, including their own parents. I remember a time when children, even young adults, were in the presence of older adults, they would not curse. But if they cursed and later realized that an adult was in their presence, they immediately apologized. They were ashamed of their behavior. This type of self-discipline or even the apology is seldom seen or heard today.

Why is that? Why are our children committing crimes at all hours of the night? Why is an eleven-year-old out of the house hanging out with friends at 11pm? Is there not an established curfew in our homes regarding when our children should be home? I remember having to be home before the street lights came on. Why is it okay with Mamas today that our children sag their pants or wear too-short or too-revealing clothing in our presence?

Now don't get me wrong, wearing inappropriate clothing is not a new trend. But what happened to the child sneaking those clothes in and out of the house and changing in and out of them before they returned home? As parents, are we holding our end of the commitment? Are we encouraging our girls to respect themselves and our boys to respect and consider others? Are we being THE parent?

Secondly, I understand earning a living. Some of us are in situations where we are the only income earners in our homes. I get it. But who's raising our children while we're working? Who's responsible for them when we are away? Additionally, what exactly are Mamas working for? Are we working to provide the basic essentials like shelter, food and clothing for our family? Or are we working for luxuries like a huge flat-screen television and cable in every room of the home, name brand clothing and shoes for our children, the nails, the hair-do for ourselves and our daughters, the newest video game, the latest ride? Most times when we are attempting to satisfy ourselves and our children with these luxury items, it is mostly to compensate for what we think is lacking in the home – like the presence of the other parent. It requires that we work more than one job, which means our children are left alone more often, without our guidance. A lot of times, we end up paying far more for the luxuries than they are worth because our children are raising themselves; left with too much unsupervised time on their hands and opportunities to connect with people, places, and things of which we do not approve. Are we being THE parent?

Thirdly, I understand needing a break. I understand wanting to pamper yourself. Parenting is hard work and full of sacrifices. As moms, we give and we give and we give. We give to the point that we do without some of the things we want–and for some of us, we even stop wanting anything. We're simply trying to provide and survive. At certain stages of our children's lives, we can't even go to the bathroom without being interrupted or, at a minimum, followed.

Parenting can be overwhelming and just difficult. But once you become a parent, raising your child must become the priority of your life. The sacrifices just come with parenting and for as long as you are a parent, there will be sacrifices. Have you noticed the number of recent news reports of mothers leaving their children unattended or attended by someone who wasn't dependable or responsible? So again, I ask the question that I began with, "Are we being THE parent?"

***Crown Coordination***: I often encourage moms of young children to raise their child(ren) with the end in mind. What do I mean by this? Start teaching them your desired attributes and expectations early. For example, if a behavior is considered and encouraged as cute at the toddler stage (like a child who thinks it's funny to kick people) don't get upset with your child when they are age ten and still kicking people. My suggestion: If the kicking behavior is not what you want your child to develop into a habit, stop the kicking behavior when it starts. It's better to teach your child what's expected of them from the beginning than to have to un-teach a learned undesirable behavior later on in life. (It is believed by many theorists that children learn their core values by age ten.)

Additionally, if we want our child to be respectful to others in life, we begin to teach our child to be respectful of others in the home while they are young. There is absolutely nothing wrong with a child saying *"Thank you"* and *"Please"* at home with the people they share the house with. Home is where it all starts. Now, being respectful goes beyond saying *"Yes, ma'am"* and *"No, ma'am"* to adults. It's a good thing if that's what you want them to say but it is not the only measure of respectful behavior. Being respectful is demonstrated when we are courteous, polite and considerate of others.

Parenting requires that we set the standards for our children while they are in our homes, and hopefully, our children will take what they have learned in our homes and live productively in society. This will include setting boundaries, allowing our children to experience the consequences of their actions, and teaching our children morals and ethics. Understand that in most cases, what we teach our children is what our children will teach their children and their children will teach their children. Our actions today will heavily influence many generations to come. Sister, YOU Matter!

Next, I want to spend some time addressing some very essential tenets of parenting. As already stated, parenting is much more than simply meeting the physical needs of our children. It's about nurturing the entire child: the physical, emotional, intellectual, and spiritual components of our children. We can nurture them by affirming them, loving them, disciplining them, being honest with them about our mistakes, listening to them, and giving our best to them regardless of the circumstances.

## Affirming Our Children

### *Catch Them Being Good*

Would you treat someone outside of your home the way you treat your children? The words you say, the tone you use when you're upset with your children–are those the same words and tones you would use with your co-workers or children you work with in the community (like mentoring programs, church, etc.) when you're upset with them?

Some of us curse at our children, call them degrading names, and scream at them so much that it's common-place in our homes. So when our children observe us speaking differently to others outside of the home, they're trying to determine which is the real person: the person they witness at home or the person they and others see portrayed in public. When we do this, we are modeling hypocrisy and disrespect towards others. We are also possibly showing our child that we don't value them as much as we value the people outside of our homes.

***Crown Coordination:*** If we allow them to, our children will teach us a lot about ourselves. Their behaviors are most-times a reflection of how we behave and who we are in the home. If we use shame and guilt in the home with words like "Girl, you are so stupid, just dumb!" Guess what? Our children will use those same methods (not necessarily the exact words) outside of the home.

Ok, so these types of words are not used in your home. That's good. But do your actions convey the same message? For instance, are you praising your child when he/she gets it right? Or do you tend to focus more on punishing them when they get it wrong? Please understand that positive and appropriate discipline is required but I want to encourage you to look for opportunities to really pay attention and reward your children when they get it right. Rewards are not always monetary. They could be as simple as a hug, a high five, a handwritten "I love you," a "thank you," or an "I'm so proud of you" note—or even just a smile.

Sister, our children are eager to please us—even as adults—and want our attention.  They'll get it from us however they can—positively or negatively. So, if the only time our child gets attention from us is when he/she messes up, then guess what. We're going to see a lot of mess-ups from our child. I read once that for each positive statement a child receives, he or she is given 14 negative ones. Would you bet on 1:14 odds for success? So now I challenge you to change those odds and set your child up for success by shifting those negative words to positive ones. I like to say "Catch them being good."

Think about your child, even your adult child (each one of them if you have more than one), and something they did right today or recently. Now write it down.

_____

_____

_____

_____

Next, be intentional about rewarding them for getting it right or doing it well. I encourage you not to spend money on the reward.

*Quality Time*

Another way to affirm our children is by spending quality time with them. Have you noticed the number of electronics at the dinner table? (Or is a more appropriate question, *what* dinner table?) With phones, tablets, computers  and hand-held gaming systems, there does not seem to be much conversation among the diners at the table. Everybody seems preoccupied with whatever device they're holding in their hands. The hand-held devices seem to get more of our attention than the people living in the same house with us.

Have you ever thought about how that may make your family members feel? Doesn't it feel good to you when someone invites you to lunch or dinner, just to spend quality time with you? When we get the opportunity to catch up with old friends, we so look forward to the uninterrupted time with them, don't we?

Guess what? Our children look forward to this type of time with us as well. As human beings, we need to feel like we belong. That's probably one of the most important functions of the family unit—to create a sense of belonging for each member of the family. Trust me, if we don't create this sense of safety and belonging for our children in the home, they will find it elsewhere. It becomes a void that they try to fill with all sorts of activities and friends.  In most cases, these "fillers" are not our ideal outlets for our children, and not the friends and/or activities we would encourage our children to engage with or in.

**Crown Coordination:** So how do we juggle quality time with our children into our already hectic schedules?  Here are two suggestions that could be good starting points:

1. Ask your child about the activities of their day. Ask them to tell you one interesting activity about their day. Ask them about their friends at school or how (sports, music, etc.) practice went. It's not an interrogation, it's showing interest in them as a person.

2. Identify activities that are common for all of the family members. Designate a time as "family time" and set ground rules, like no hand-held devices during this activity together. The first of these events could be discussing and planning the "family time" concept and activities and hearing your children's suggestions. Be sure to take these suggestions into consideration. The plan is more likely to be accepted if everyone is given the opportunity to actively participate in the planning and development.

Let's use eating meals as an example. Since everyone in the house has to eat, schedule at least one meal a week where everybody eats together. It could be breakfast on Saturday morning, dinner and a movie on Friday night, brunch or lunch on Sunday. This does not have to be expensive. For example, dinner and a movie could take place at home, eating a home cooked meal and watching a family appropriate movie (cable, streaming service or DVD) together. It's doable and will take some planning but the rewards will be well worth it.

Our children will feel like they are just as important to us as the person or content on the other end of the electronic device that seems to command so much of our undivided attention. Sister, YOU Matter!

Identify and list how you currently spend quality uninterrupted time with your children.

_____

_____

_____

 Identify and list how you would *like* to spend quality uninterrupted with your children.

_____

_____

_____

 Plan it.
- What:
- When:
- How often:
- Where:
- Time:
- Ground rules:

I Love You

{ "I never knew how much love my heart could hold until someone called me 'mommy.'"

**Author Unknown** }

So often I hear parents preparing to have their first child say something like, "I look forward to having someone who will love me unconditionally." I'm sure I thought it too, even if I didn't say it out loud. I hate to be the bearer of the disappointing news but this is most likely *not* how you're going to feel throughout most of this parenting journey especially during the early and teen years. There may even be times when your child tells you that he/she does not love you. This usually happens when they can't get their way. And, guess what? At this time, truth be told, you may not be liking him/her too much either because of their behavior at that moment. The unconditional love part comes from YOU; and YOU give it to your child.

***Crown Coordination:*** Our children need to know that we love them but more importantly, they need to hear us *say* it to them often and for no reason at all. Just out of nowhere, you should tell your children you love them. You should tell them often. Every once and while, tell them you love them and/or are proud of them for no reason at all. If they ask, "For what?" You say, "*Just for being you!*" and say it with a smile.

Honestly, for most of us, isn't this the way we felt when we first held our "little bundle of joy" in our arms? We loved them just because. We were proud of them just because. We thought he or she was the best baby in the world--just because. Communicate the "just because" to your child as much as possible. Don't wait until after they've done something good to be the only time they hear these "just because" sentiments. Your child needs to hear them often and "just because."

"But I show them that I love them." Yes, you do and that is good. Your child is very grateful for those actions but they also need to hear it and hear it often. Doesn't it make you feel good when someone you admire and/or respect tells you they love you? It has the same effect on our children. Their faces start glowing, their eyes become full of life, their mood even lightens— just because their mama told them she loves them "just because."

A lot of times we confuse buying gifts and material things for our children as showing love. Yes, that can be an expression of our love to them but that should not be the only way we show it. What happens when we can no longer afford to buy the gifts? What happens when our child makes mistakes that our money can't buy them out of? Does our child still know that we love them unconditionally?

Identify the last time you told your child(ren) "I love you" or "I'm proud of you" just because. Commit to telling your child "I love you" at least once a day. This should be a random act and this random once-a-day act should be completed in addition to telling them as a reward for a good act/behavior.

_____

_____

_____

## Controlling Your Child

> *"Controlling your child is like trying to clench the wind in your fists."*
>
> **B. C. Raines**

I don't care how hard you try, you cannot control your child. I repeat: you *cannot* control your child. Now, I have to digress a little here. You may see a child running wildly in a store and ask yourself, "Would that mama control her child, please?" I'm not talking about that type of control; that's discipline and discipline is an essential responsibility of parenting. Now, using this same example: If the mother controlled the child, the child would not have been running wildly through the store in the first place. Secondly, the child would have most likely been asleep or at least completely silent during the entire store event. Thirdly, not only would the child have been silent in the store but during the entire trip to *and* from the store as well. Now, how likely are these ideal scenarios to happen on every single trip to the store? *Not likely* at all because we don't control our children. Do you see the difference between discipline and control?

Now, we can influence our child's actions to please us—we call this discipline—but we cannot control them. Hang with me, here's an illustration of what I mean: Think about any remotely controlled device. The device only works when you do something to it, and most times, it only does what you push the corresponding button to tell it to do, right? As long as you don't touch the TV's remote control, it stays just as it is. If you want to change the channel, adjust the volume, etc., you physically have to do something to cause the change, right? What button do you we push for our child to respond a certain way? Is there a volume button? A "no temper tantrum" button? An "eat all of the food on your plate" button? A "stop running in the house" button? A "go to bed" button? A "be home by your curfew" button? There isn't one, is there?

Remember the terrible twos, threes and fours? I like to add the threes and fours because, for me, the "terribles" did not abruptly stop on my child's third birthday—not sure about you…Those times were so "terrible" because our children were learning that they were independent from us. They could move their arms, legs, and tongues; remove their clothing, shake their heads and touch things without us. They were also learning the boundaries. See, our children have their own minds and capabilities and will use them. As a matter of fact, we teach them to use them. We just don't like it when they use them contrary to our expectations or desires.

So what do you do? Change the batteries? Get a new remote? Take the child back to store from where you purchased them? No, we parent. We give them "options" and positive or not-so-positive rewards to accompany those options. It looks something like this: If you (the child) do it this way, you get responses that you like. If you (the child) do it that way, you get responses that you don't like.

***Crown Coordination:*** Developing a different outlook regarding this "power struggle" with your child can decrease our stress and frustration as a parent. This could be your opportunity to be creative with your parenting style. One suggestion is to begin by identifying what your child likes. This is crucial, especially if you have more than one child, because the reward system that may have worked with one child, may not work at all with your other children. You could end up encouraging an undesired behavior in one of your children because he/she likes the reward received although the other child does not. For example, time-out while sitting in a chair may not affect all of your children the same way. Identifying these will help you give rewards (positive and not so positive) that are unique to his or her "likes."

As I close this segment, I have to remind you that children are not "good" or "bad," their *behaviors* are. Label the behaviors as "good" or "bad," if you choose to but not the child. Learn to separate the undesirable behavior from the child. The child committing the undesired behavior is the same child that you just praised for "getting it right," or you told "I love you" just because. Yes, it's the same child, I promise. It's just that this specific behavior is not pleasant or appropriate and you should parent appropriately at these times. Be careful how you label your child. Also, be careful of the labels you allow others to assign to your child, especially the authority figures in your child's life. What you (or others) call your child is exactly what your child will respond to.

<u>Oops</u>

> "You can learn great things from your mistakes when you aren't busy denying them."
>
> ### *The 7 Habits of Highly Effective People*

Mistakes will happen. We are human and we will make mistakes while parenting–and they won't stop when our child(ren) becomes an adult. We'll make some different mistakes then.

***Crown Coordination:*** One of the most liberating experiences for me as a mother was when I could apologize to my child when I made a mistake. I don't remember the details; he was a toddler then. But I do remember the relief in his eyes when I sincerely apologized for accusing him of doing something that he did not do. My apology changed our relationship. I didn't have to keep acting like I had all the answers when I knew I didn't. In retrospect, I was behaving more like a territorial tyrant than a nurturing mother. I guess I was having my own "terrible twos through fours" episode.

Additionally, it helped him to accept making mistakes of his own. He felt comfortable enough to process them with me and we worked through them together. I prefer teaching him more appropriate problem resolution skills rather than him trying to figure them out all on his own. Or even worse, having him thinking that he or other human beings can't make mistakes. Mistakes happen. They are an inevitable, yet essential, part of life. An important lesson that our children (and even we) must learn is that it's what we do after the mistakes that make the difference. Our response to the mistakes is what helps or hurts us–not so much the mistake itself.

Identify a time when you needed to apologize to your child for acting in a way that was not "Crown" worthy. Maybe you used some words out of anger that you should not have used. Maybe you accused them of something that you later realized they did not do.

_____

_____

_____

_____

_____

_____

_____

_____

_____

_____

_____

_____

Listening to Your Child

"The first duty of love is to listen."
*Paul Tillich*

I live in the Deep South and it gets pretty hot during the summer months. "Pretty hot" is an expression we Southerners use. Believe me, there is absolutely nothing "pretty" about this hot. Try to be pretty if you want to during one of these "pretty hot" days and you'll most likely look a "pretty hot" mess. I think this is our polite Southern way of saying, it's *extremely* hot. Maybe we're a little embarrassed to tell others how really hot it is because they may not want to visit us during these "pretty hot" days. I don't know, that's just my guess. I digress. So as a mom, I thought the best summer attire for my child included sandals. I mean, gym shoes and socks in the summer? In the Deep South? What "good" parent, especially a mama, allows that?

My child was attending preschool daily and it was my job to ensure that he dressed well–with color coordinated outfits and cute comfortable shoes, right? And from my perspective, only sandals would complete the look I was trying to achieve for this young person that I was trying to teach not only how to dress but dress well for the season. Plus, he's representing the family name (it's another one of those Deep South traditions.) So I felt I had been "more than flexible enough" with my child regarding the sandal issue. I had spent money – good, hard-earned money, mind you–summer after summer after summer on those cute sandals that would really make my son's summer outfits so adorable but he had been so adamant about not wearing them. (Sigh.) I finally asked, "Why don't you wear your sandals, it's summertime?" His response: "Because rocks get in my shoes when I play outside."

That made perfect sense. I had a quick flashback to having the same dilemma when I was younger but I just learned to adapt. I never thought to wear a different shoe. I must admit, I felt "not so smart" after his response. But guess what? I heard him and I stopped pressing the issue (at least for the preschool attendance days.) I also saved myself some frustration and some money.

**Crown Coordination:** I think sometimes as parents, especially mothers, we want so desperately to paint a picture of having it all together and we make the parenting experience a lot more stressful than it has to be. Parenting, in and of itself, is difficult and stressful but some of the pressure we've added due to feeling like we have to have all of the answers. We think that we have to have it all thought-out and act like we have it all together. Our children, as I mentioned earlier, have their own minds and also their own ideas and their own ways of thinking about things. Our way doesn't have to be the *only* way in all of the situations. When we allow our children to have a voice in our homes, it encourages creative thinking, development of effective problem solving skills, and the freedom to learn from mistakes in our safe home environment.

Due to the technology advancements in our society today, we must consider creating mentally and emotionally healthy, as well as physically healthy and safe, home environments or our children may be more likely to become prey in a vicious cyber world. We are losing so many of our children to what I refer to as the "cyber underworld." The cyber underworld's audience will hear them and allow them to express their concerns and feelings without judgment, without condemnation, and will offer very attractive and affirming options to our children.

So, we can choose to parent with the traditional "Because I said so," response commonly used by our parents and grandparents (and sometimes that may be the most appropriate response, even now). However, we may not like the options that our children choose in response to this "traditional" method if it's used all of the time with no inclusive alternatives. Remember, creating safety and a sense of belonging in our child's life is a basic life need that should be met in our homes.

Identify and list the areas where you need to listen to your children more.

_____

_____

_____

How will you listen?

_____

_____

_____

When will you listen?

_____

_____

_____

🪶 How often will you listen?

_____

_____

_____

🪶 Identify a time when you have listened to your child. How did your child react? How did it make you feel? Was your perspective changed as a result of listening to your child?

_____

_____

_____

## I Can't Teach Him How to Be a Man

Nope, you (the woman) cannot. Period. The end. Conversation over. Hopefully this declaration takes some weight off of your shoulders, relieves some of the pressure and removes some of the guilt you may have been carrying if you are single and parenting a son. But this declaration does not relinquish us of our responsibility to parent him. Yep, that's still our responsibility.

I've heard (and have been told) this one statement a lot: "You can't teach him how to be a man." I've wallowed in it, too. See, I am single and I've been raising my son as a single parent since he was two months old (he's a teenager now.) I tell you, facing the reality that I would have to raise him without his dad was difficult and sometimes left me very angry. How was I, a woman, supposed to equip him, a maturing (and quite handsome, I might add) boy, for the world as a man?

Yes, I had a living Dad and brothers to help but they did not live in the house with me and my son. My son did not have someone in the home on a daily basis that he could model regarding the man's view of the world. You know a man's view is very different from a woman's–my son has definitely taught me that one.

Sometimes it felt unfair...not just for me but more importantly, for my son. This wasn't the way it was supposed to be. This definitely was not the plan I had mapped out. There were also times I felt very guilty and even spent a lot of time being embarrassed and resenting the whole "single parent" scenario. Single parenting was (and still can be) very overwhelming at times. But one day, the bright light went off for me: many women have done this (single parenting) successfully before me with fewer resources than I have. If they can make it, certainly I can.

Sister, contrary to what the media would have us believe, single parenthood did not just start. For example, fathers have been dying prematurely for years, leaving women to raise the children in their absence. If you were to look back into our American history, moms have been heads of households for a long time. During slavery times, it was not uncommon for fathers to be sold to other owners, forced to leave the plantation, or even killed—leaving behind women to raise their children without the father in the home or anywhere nearby for that matter. During wars, American men would leave their wives and children never to return. However, the children raised during these prominent times in our history became famed physicians, attorneys, scientists, musicians, actors, entrepreneurs, businessmen, athletes, etc. That's what single parenthood produced—great influential men (and women) who changed the world on so many levels. And guess what...it still can.

**Crown Coordination:** So, back to my situation...I began to identify the things I *could* teach my son. If you are on this same journey, I encourage you to do the same. Focusing on what you *can't* teach him will drain you of your emotional resources to parent him. Teach him what you can—teach him how to be a gentleman. Teach him to be responsible. Teach him to love himself. Teach him to turn negatives into positives. Teach him about forgiveness, especially regarding the absence of his father. (This one will be so important because he's going to be someone's father someday and you don't want him carrying this unresolved stuff into your grandchild's life—it becomes a vicious continuous cycle.)

So no, you can't teach him how to be a man but you can love him unconditionally and nurture and validate him. You can build him up and prepare him as best you can for a world that will try to break him down. This validation is one of the most powerful areas of your influence in his life.

*NOTE: Sister, **PLEASE** don't go "find" a man to put over your son (or any of your children, for that matter) because you feel that your son needs a role model in the home. Having the wrong male influence over your son can be potentially more detrimental to your son than having no in-home role model at all.*

Believe it or not, you are capable of modeling the essential characteristics he needs: love, joy, peace, patience, kindness towards others and gentleness towards himself, goodness, faithfulness, self-control, and contentment. The modeling of these characteristics will nurture and imprint on your son the productive attributes of honesty, integrity, dependability and hard work. See Sister, you–the mother–have all that you need. Sister, YOU Matter!

Identify what you can teach your son and the reason for teaching him. See the example below.

| Activity | Reason |
|---|---|
| Cooking | So he can cook for himself |
| _____ | _____ |
| _____ | _____ |
| _____ | _____ |
| _____ | _____ |
| _____ | _____ |

Identify resources available to you to expose your son to positive male role models.

_____
_____
_____
_____

# Children Live What They Learn

*Author Unknown*

If children live with criticism,
they learn to condemn.

If children live with hostility,
they learn to fight.

If children live with fear,
they learn to be apprehensive.

If children live with pity,
they learn to feel sorry for themselves.

If children live with ridicule,
they learn to feel shy.

If children live with jealousy,
they learn to feel envy.

If children live with shame,
they learn to feel guilty.

If children live with encouragement,
they learn confidence.

If children live with tolerance,
they learn patience.

If children live with praise,
they learn appreciation.

If children live with acceptance,
they learn to love.

If children live with approval,
they learn to like themselves.

If children live with recognition,
they learn it is good to have a goal.

If children live with sharing,
they learn generosity.

If children live with honesty,
they learn truthfulness.

If children live with fairness,
they learn justice.

If children live with kindness and consideration,
they learn respect.

If children live with security,
they learn to have faith in themselves and in those about them.

If children live with friendliness,
they learn the world is a nice place in which to live.

## Mentor

> "The greatest good you can do for others is not just to share your riches but reveal to them theirs."
>
> **Benjamin Disraeli**

A few years ago, popular athletes began boasting, "I'm not a role model." It was so shocking to hear at the time because for as long as the Earth had been spinning, young people had idolized their favorite public star—an athlete, actress, actor, singer, dancer, etc. This newly-spoken sentiment began to be commonplace thinking and seemingly gave stars an excuse to behave however they chose without being held accountable by the public for their actions.

Sister, the reality is that we are role models (famous or not) and more than that, we should want to be accountable to other young people (both in years and maturity) that are observing us. And believe me, someone is always, ALWAYS observing: your mom, your sister, your aunt, your niece, your friend, your co-worker, your church member... yes, even your daughter. The mentoring role should not be taken lightly and you don't have to search hard for someone who needs someone they can look up to.

I read once, and I agree, that the best way to help yourself is to help someone else. Be the gentle guide that you needed but may not have had access to. Be the quiet whisper that speaks bold encouragement and exhibits calmness, strength and perseverance in a world that celebrates loudness, rudeness and self-serving and self-defeating behaviors. Be someone's cheerleader in their game of life.

Sister, you have what it takes to encourage the next person to take the next step. Your nieces are taking notes. Your neighbors are inspecting.

Your co-workers, your boss, the security guard, the store cashier...are all checking you out. The listing could go on and on. Sister, YOU Matter!

Someone else needs you to be their hand up, their light, their high-five, their "You go girl!" Sister, yes, YOU. Sister, YOU Matter!

I don't know about you but when I think of the word mentoring, I envision a young professional woman gently coaching a young girl/teen. The coaching could be in the form of tutorial support, a sounding board for the younger sister or an imparting of wisdom in various matters of life. I also immediately think of this as a volunteer sign-up opportunity.

But did you know that you are mentoring each time you rise out of bed? Someone else is taking notice of you: your spouse (if you're married) and children (if you have them) in the home, your neighbors in your community, the people on your job, the personnel at school (yours and/or your child's), your church members, even strangers in the mall or at the grocery store. Yes, you're an example to someone all the time. Mentoring is an active exchange that occurs constantly and consistently and most times without your consent or physically signing up for the job.

**Crown Coordination:** I like this quote from an unknown source about mentoring: *"Mentor: Someone whose hindsight can become your foresight."* You may also be mentored to (or provide mentoring) at any phase of your life. As the requirements of our roles shift and change (and with time, they certainly will change) we could learn from others who have already been where we are or where we are headed, just as we do for those coming behind us. You may be watching someone else for guidance regarding what's appropriate in a particular season of your life. Also, there could be multiple mentors in your life at one time in different areas, each pouring into you just as you are pouring into someone else or multiple others.

Mentoring is not always based on age; it's more about the maturity of the people involved in the exchange than the peoples' ages. The older woman (by age) can learn from the younger-aged woman just as well as the younger-aged woman can learn from the older ones. There may be an area in your life where you are more mature than a person who is older than you are. It becomes your obligation to model what you know -regardless of her age. It's the other person's responsibility, whether they are a girl, teen, or a woman, to be receptive. Sister, YOU Matter!

> "Successful people turn everyone who can help them into sometime mentors!"
> *John Crosby*

## Wife

Marriage is beautiful. I think it is one of the most beautiful human relationships known to mankind. The beauty is in two people, with all of their differences, choosing to live life as one, in harmony with another person; sharing time, love, life, and all that is to come.

Help-meet. The Better half. Wifey. Bride. Spouse. Life Partner. This title is coveted and yet the role is so taken for granted. We throw the title around like it's a limp dirty rag that's of no use after a few good washes. A lot of people use the words "wedding" and "marriage" interchangeably; and when we do that, it tends to cause a lot of problems in the marriage.

<u>The Wedding</u>

The wedding is usually a one-day event at a specified time, shared with specified people. Women tend to spend a lot of money (that we may not have) and time on the wedding not considering or even understanding the possible irreparable damage we could be causing the marriage–you know, that union *after* the wedding; the *forever* part of the ceremony; the *"'til death do us part"* element of the vows. It's so easy to lose focus of the marriage when planning our wedding because it's such a big day. For most of us, we've known for such long time how we've imagined this day. This wedding ideal is so serious that there are some women who, even after many years of a successful marriage, feel that their marriage isn't valid in some sense because they did not have the wedding of their dreams. (Yes, this includes even those who had a wedding but maybe it just wasn't the version they'd dreamed about all of their single lives.)

Sister, it's just one day. It's just the beginning. The wedding can come later in the marriage if it continues to be that important to you. If the big wedding is what you want, go for it; but keep your focus on the marriage. If, for whatever reason, you didn't have or even want a wedding, or if you didn't have the wedding of your dreams, it's okay. Just keep the focus on the marriage–the two people vowing to love each other through sickness and health; for richer or for poorer.

***Crown Coordination:*** Are you the same person during the wedding planning as the woman he asked to marry him? I have seen television shows that exploit brides-to-be, turning the wedding preparation into such an undesirable event that family members and friends are offended. Sometimes, even the actual anticipated marriage itself is canceled because the bride-elect's Crown got lost in the wedding planning. Remember, you are more than this one day. This one day does not define you. I have seen (and been told of) numerous marriages (expensive wedding and not) ending fairly quickly, largely because of money issues and lack of communication regarding each other's finances. These 'money' conversations need to start before the "I do" ceremony. I think a wise question we may need to ask ourselves, prior to any spending on the wedding, "Is this debt (financial and emotional) something my marriage can afford?"

## The Marriage

Marriage–the forever vow made during the wedding event–on its own will have its ups and downs. For most marriages, there will be more ups than downs. Marriage requires a lot of hard work. It's your choice to stay or go but just be sure that whatever choice you make, it's your choice. Other people outside of the relationship will give you advice regarding what they consider is your best choice but please know that only you should make the choice that you think is best for you and your situation. You, and you alone, will have to live with the outcome of your decision. Some of us give up too quickly and some of us stay way too long in our marriages but it's about choosing.

Remember that chat we had about submission in Chapter 4, choosing to fight or flow. Submission is definitely an essential component of the marriage relationship. Now, I'm not encouraging anyone to stay in an unhealthy relationship, that's a decision that only you, and you alone, can make. However, please understand that domestically violent relationships are centered on power and control of the abuser towards the abused, not love. I repeat: an abusive relationship, especially a physically abusive one, is not based on love. If you are the perpetrator of violence in your marriage, or if you are being physically abused in your marriage, please seek professional help.

Maybe you've been married a long time (or what seems like a long time) and he gets on your nerves because he's not the man he should be (and for some of us, he's not who we thought we were marrying). I know you "can do badly all by yourself." I know you "can do this on your own." I know you're tired. You've had enough. You're just sick of him. Sound familiar? Sadly, this talk about our husbands and marriages is more common than you think.

***Crown Coordination:*** I want you to remember that marriage is about the *two* of you–and you have faults, too. Yes, you may have gotten better in some areas but you still have some work to do, too. Marriage won't ever be 50/50–one person will ALWAYS give more than the other, it just may be in different areas of the marriage. That's the beauty and the compliment of marriage–there is someone else taking the walk with you.

You don't have to be strong in every area of the marriage. There's someone else who's equipped and strong in some of the areas that you may not be so strong in. Now, let him be strong. Believe it or not, his strength in some areas is what first attracted you to him. So let him be just that–allow him to flex his muscle in that area of your marriage. Yes, expect some mistakes. Expect that he may not do it exactly the way you would have done it. But just allow him to use his strengths in the marriage, too.

## The Thermostat

Have you considered being the change you want to see in your husband? For example, if you want a kinder husband, are your actions and words kind towards him? If you want a concerned husband, do you show concern towards him? I encourage you to model what you want from your husband instead of complaining about and/or magnifying what he's not. For instance, when his words hurt you, could you try to respond in a way that you would want to hear him respond to you? Now, don't do this expecting anything from him in return, you can't change him. You are choosing (submission act) to respond this way in an effort to regulate the atmosphere in your home. Just because he cheats, it does not justify you cheating, too. You, the woman–the Crown–set the standard in your home.

***Crown Coordination:*** Can you find some positives in your husband and really praise him for those attributes? Can you catch him getting it right? When you catch him getting it right, can you mention it to him? "Hey, thanks for taking the trash out." "I really appreciated you checking with me first before you invited the guys over the other day." "Thanks for washing the car for me, it's really a big help."

For so long, you may have been focused on and communicated the negative about him or what he does wrong, or doesn't do, that maybe he's tuned you out. Do you realize that if you keep telling a person what they can't or aren't doing, they're more likely to keep doing it? He's probably feeling just like you–unappreciated, neglected, unloved and exhausted. So encourage your husband. Use your words to speak life into your husband and your marriage. Choose those 'sweet nothings' to whisper in his ear like you used to do. You know, for some of us, our actions and words will actually lead our husbands to live better and healthier lives. Yes, you have that much influence potential. But you have to use it wisely. Sister, YOU Matter!

> "I find the best way to love someone is not to change them, but instead, help them reveal the greatest version of themselves."
>
> ***Steve Maraboli***
>
> "Unapologetically You: Reflections on Life and the Human Experience"

## Getting It Back

You remember before you married, you cleared your calendar for him. I mean, for most of us, we dropped everything–our friend girls, our trip to the mall...we may have even left work early or not gone to work at all. We definitely made sure the children were taken care of, etc. Is he still that important to you? Do you still give him your undivided attention? Do you still get giddy when you anticipate seeing or hearing from him? Do you remember those days? Are those still your days? If not, what happened? How do you get those days back?

*Crown Coordination:* You work at it. You do your part. You can't do his part and you shouldn't do your part to in an attempt to manipulate him into anything. For starters, schedule a date with him. Your date can be as extravagant or simple as you desire. It's just your time with him alone. No children. No friends. No tablets. No phones. No distractions. Just the two of you. Sister, give your marriage your all. If you were going to "step out," you'd have to give that relationship your undivided attention, so invest that same time, effort and energy into your marriage. One of the most gratifying outcomes, is knowing you did your very best to honor your vows. Sister, YOU Matter!

**Dating Relationship Partner**

I AM the Crown. I AM the Crown. I AM the Crown. I AM the Crown.

If at no other time in your life you remember this, please remember "I AM the Crown" during the dating phase of your life. You are the Crown. You are the catch. You are to be caught. He should find you and then you can choose him.

Boo. Girlfriend. Significant other. Babe. Fiancé. Such terms of endearment. Hearing those makes us feel so special, so wanted, so loved. But I have to ask...why are you dating? What's your purpose for dating? Are you dating for the next dinner and a movie? Are you dating because you don't want to be alone? Are you dating in hopes of marrying? Are you dating just to have something to do? Your motive for dating will also greatly influence how you date and who you select to date. It's your time, use it wisely.

I think we're cheating ourselves out of such a great, sweet and innocent experience in our lives when we don't savor the dating phase. This should be his time to show you how much he thinks of you, to show you what life will be like with him, his time to persuade you that he is the best man for you. It shouldn't be the other way around.

We spend so much of our energy during this phase of our life trying to convince him that we're the best for him. It's all connected to that

Crown image—when we don't really understand our worth or our value, we feel like we have to prove something to everyone that comes our way.

I spent a large portion of my life waiting to be "picked." Remember in the Introduction, I explained that I felt unloved, so to be picked...wow! I thought I had to flow with the person who picked me (you know, make lemonade out of the lemons), not realizing that I got to choose. The order of things: he finds, I choose. So he should be the one proving himself to me, not me to him—but I had to get there.

Sister, a man knows what he wants before he meets you. You would be surprised at how many don't approach you because they see your Crown and know that all they are trying to do is conquer the next conquest. Be thankful that he skipped you. You are the Crown and if you don't know who you are during this dating phase of your life, don't expect him to know who you are. He will treat you exactly the way you allow him to treat you. You deserve the very best. You are the very best...remember, you are the Crowning glory of the creation. You deserve the calls, the dinners, the extra special attention, the flowers, the walks in the park, the utmost respect. You deserve it all.

Remember, love is an action word. If he tells you he loves you, then let him also show you. He should be ready to put your needs before his own. He should want to give you his best self. He should always look out for you and your best interests...if he says he loves you and means it, he'll want to protect you and show you to the world. You'll be the spark in his eye. You'll be the missing link in his chain, the sugar in his Kool-Aid. He will enjoy showing you how much you mean to him. He understands that you are a treasure that he's found and will want to keep you.

***Crown Coordination:*** Let him pamper you. Let him show you what life will be like with him, if you choose him. While dating, pay attention to how he treats his family, especially the living female relatives in his life: his mom, grandmother, his sister, his aunts and even his daughter(s). It could tell you a lot about how he shows care and concern for women in general. Sister, if he is unfaithful to you while dating, you shouldn't be surprised if he's unfaithful to you if you choose to marry him. Pay attention. This should be the time when he's being his very best for you. Pay attention.

## Your Dessert

Some advice that some of my male friends have given me over the years: "Keep your cookies in your pocket." (I call it dessert. It can be cookies, pies, ice cream, etc.—your choice.) I know this seems impossible because so much of our dating pivots on physical intimacy. We can't wait to experience him, to see what he's working with *('cause we ain't trying to waste our time if he ain't working with nothing!)* and he can't wait to experience you either, his next encounter. We give so much of ourselves way too early in the dating experience. And because we give so much, we are crushed when things don't end the way we anticipated and we forget that we get "to choose."

Slow things down. Get to know him and let him get to know you "with your cookies in your pocket." Once you give your dessert away, you become connected to him in ways that a man and woman become connected to each other after marriage. It's not just a physical act; it's also very emotional and spiritual. Be selective about who you allow to enter you. Have you ever noticed that after the "dessert" event, most times we start asking the desperate questions (at least to ourselves, if not to him): "So are we in a relationship?" "Where is this relationship going?" "Will I see you again?"

Sister, these are the questions we should know the answers to BEFORE the dessert event. My advice: It's best to wait...because after, it's too late. *Your dessert is gone and you can't get it back. Sister, YOU Matter!*

> "The most painful thing is losing yourself in the process of loving someone too much, and forgetting that you are special too."
>
> ***Author Unknown***

## Dating...His Children?

If you are dating a man who has a child or children with another woman (or women), pay close attention to how he treats his children; it will tell you a lot about the type of man he is. Encourage him to provide for and spend quality time with his child. Additionally, if he's not consistently providing for and/or spending time with his children, I suggest that you really ask him about it. These actions could be telling you more about him than you realize.

Sister, here's something for you to consider: Instead of perceiving his child as an extension of their mother and/or a threat to your relationship with your current "Boo," see the child (yes, his child) as a reflection of you–the 'child' part of you. Wasn't it important to you to see and spend time with your dad? Regardless of if he showed up or not, it was still important to you. His child feels the same way.

***Crown Coordination:*** Here's where your self-worth (Crown) really radiates who you are–use your authority, your influence, to empower the next generation to expect our men to make the right choices regarding our children. I say "our children" because your child someday may be on the receiving end of this action from another woman; the woman that your now–but could-be "used-to-be" Boo–will be connected to.

The child's mom (or her previous relationship with the guy you're dating) is none of your business. If he chooses to be with her, let him go. There's nothing wrong with you because a person chooses someone else instead of you. If he chooses her over you, it's his loss, not yours.

You are still the Crown. You are still You (hopefully with your dessert still in your possession). He didn't see your value. You were just too much treasure for him, he didn't know what he had and certainly did not know what to do with what he had found in you.  It's okay. Be willing to let people go when they want to go and learn to be content with it. Letting them go just means you are one step closer to your goal; for the dating phase, you're one "man" closer to *the* man for you. It is much better to have experienced this now instead of later, after you have invested much more time and energy into the relationship. Again, he finds–you choose.

> "If a person wants to be a part of your life, they will make an obvious effort to do so.  Think twice before reserving a space in your heart for people who do not make an effort to stay."
>
> ***Author Unknown***

**Neighbor**

Remember back in Chapter 3 when we explored the love purpose trait? In the love information, I mentioned: "Love others like you love yourself." The reason I focused so much on this principle is because I discovered something while writing this book: my definition of "neighbor" changed. Prior to writing this book, I thought of "neighbor" as someone outside of my home and family. However, while writing this book, my definition of neighbor became anyone other than me. For me, my neighbor, in terms of how to treat others, includes my family members living in, and outside of, my home; people in my community to include friends, neighborhood and church members, co-workers, strangers, etc. This definition would mean that all of the people affected by our various roles are indeed our neighbors. Now, our level of affection may differ depending on our relationship with the other person(s) but it's based on the same foundation: love.

Do you better understand why love has to be the foundation of our Crown? There is no way that we can effectively juggle all of our roles sincerely and genuinely without a solid, stable, yet flexible foundation of love. Love will allow us to shift from fight to flow (submission). Love will motivate us to live courageously through life's extremes. Love will help us stay when we want to go (and, in some cases, run and run quickly with no way to be found). When love is our foundation, especially loving our neighbors like we love ourselves, it makes some of our difficult choices more manageable. There are some things we'll do out of our love for others and their well-being that we wouldn't even consider doing for ourselves.

***Crown Coordination:*** In your neighbor role, I caution you not to compare yourself or your situations to others'. We don't want to exchange our satisfaction with what we have because we are wishing for (coveting) what we *think* we see of our neighbors. When we compare ourselves to others, some of those imposter traits (identified in Chapter 3) creep in—jealousy, conceit, greed, pride, anger, hatred, etc. When we engage in the comparison distraction, we begin to demean others (those that we appear to do better than) or demean ourselves because we feel we don't measure up to others.

Always keep in mind that no one's home/life situation is perfect. I repeat, no one's. Regardless of what you're told or what you think you see, you have no idea what's really going on behind the closed doors of the other person's home. We humans have perfected the art of staging: painting a "best" picture for others to see which may not be an accurate picture or the reality of the situation. I'm not saying that staging is negative or inappropriate; I am only reminding us to enjoy what we have and not yearn for what we think our eyes are seeing; our perception, regarding our neighbors. Our situation may be far better than what we "think" or imagine our neighbor's situation to be.

Do not set your heart on **<u>ANYTHING</u>** that is your neighbor's. Enough said!

*Sister, YOU Matter!*

# CHAPTER 6

"Another flaw in the human character is that everybody wants to build and nobody wants to do maintenance."

*Kurt Vonnegut, Jr.*

6

# CROWN CONSERVATION
# (CARE)

Cleaning, maintaining, the up-keep…all synonymous for more work. Just what we need, more work, right? Especially after all of that application work we just finished in the previous chapter. But to do all that we do, we have to conserve; we have to take care of ourselves, our Crowns.

We have to look after our possessions, especially the ones that are very valuable to us, if we want to conserve them. Generally, the harder we've worked for our possessions, the more valuable they are to us; for instance, our home. For most of us, most of our income goes towards paying the monthly rent or mortgage. In most cases, that large monthly payment prompts us to keep our homes clean and tidy. For those of us who own or are purchasing our homes, we know that failure to maintain the home will only cost us more later. So we try to complete preventive measures in an attempt to minimize the later (and sometimes large) expenses.

Well, now that you have selected your materials, made your Crown, and know how to use your Crown properly, are you maintaining it? Does it require cleaning? If so, how often? What type of products are needed to keep it clean? Also, different materials may require different types of cleaning aids. Be sure to use the appropriate 'cleaning' solutions for your specific setting and jewels. Cleaning with the wrong agents can be just as detrimental as not cleaning at all.

## Purpose (Why)

Do the jewel's settings need to be adjusted? Over time, the settings of our gems/jewels will need to be adjusted to continue to hold our precious jewels in place. If we are not careful and watchful, those gems/jewels may lose their luster or, even worse, we may lose the actual gems/jewels. Now those are special to you and I am sure that you don't want them to lose their luster, that you don't want to have to do without them or replace them. Replacing them could be very expensive.

## Method (How)

What does maintaining our Crown look like in everyday life? It starts with an assessment to determine the state of our Crown. Here are some questions you may want to ask to assess the state of your Crown...

- ✓ Are you still operating out of love?
- ✓ Are you still a peace maker?
- ✓ Are you still a cheerful giver?
- ✓ Is discovering your self-worth still the focus of your life? Or has it become the children, the husband, the job, the social group, church work?

This type of assessment must be routinely completed. I suggest doing this at least once a day. I know that sounds like a lot of work but we use our Crowns daily in so many different roles that the consistent assessment is crucial to maintaining the vitality of us—the Crown. Once the assessment is complete, we will have a better idea of what to use to aid in our Crown's maintenance.

**Solutions (What to Use)**

I highly recommend the cleaning agents listed below as requirements for the daily maintenance of our Crown:

- Integrity
- Forgiveness
- Thankfulness/gratefulness
- Humility
- Rest

Let's get to cleaning...

**Integrity**

> "Perhaps the surest test of an individual's integrity is his (her) refusal to do or say anything that would damage his (her) self-respect."
>
> ***Thomas S. Monson***

Sister, the key to maintaining our Crown is integrity. **Our integrity is essential for maintaining our Crown's base/foundation/setting.** Here's my definition of integrity: Integrity is doing right *especially* when no one else is looking.

Integrity is not about the other person. It's all about you. It's about you choosing (there's that submission concept again that we discussed in Chapter 4) to do right even when no else will know if you chose to do right or not. Living your life with integrity will give you the confidence to handle life's circumstances in a way that's considerate of others and an assurance of completeness about yourself. Integrity will be the catalyst for replacing our negative habits and unhealthy heart conditions that we've become so familiar with: hatred, jealousy, greed, selfishness, and others (those imposter traits we listed in Chapter 3). Integrity will also be a solid foundation for continual maintenance of those purpose traits we discussed in Chapter 3: love, joy, peace, patience, kindness, goodness, faithfulness, gentleness, self-discipline and contentment.

You know that self-worth–the Crown–I keep referring to in this book? Integrity is the basic principle of it. Integrity is the key to the continued discovery of your self-worth/value. Integrity–being true to yourself–will be the answer to the completeness you've been searching for in all of those other places:  your education, relationships, careers, and those acts we're too embarrassed to even think about anymore.

Chinua Achebe's quote sums this up best, *"One of the truest tests of integrity is its blunt refusal to be compromised."*

Integrity will be the shift that causes us to no longer focus on the next external material possession, achievement or circumstance to complete us. It will empower us to shift our focus to our inner growth and maturity and not dwell so much on the outer details. Our focus will become more about "doing" right and being right with ourselves. Now, don't get me wrong, there will still be efforts made to look good on the outside but our focus will become more about the inner beauty. As we mature the inner beauty, it will shine through us so radiantly that our natural external beauty will only be enhanced.

"If you don't have integrity, you have nothing. You can't buy it. You can have all the money in the world, but if you are not a moral and ethical person, you really have nothing."

**Henry Kravis**

**Forgiveness**

> "The mindless junk of your past crowds out opportunities and
> sets pointless limitations. Move out the junk and you create room
> for the rest of your life. Ultimately, it's not just a question of
> tidying your house; it's a question of liberating your heart."
>
> *Merlin Mann*

**Forgiveness is essential to maintaining love (affection for others) and kindness (a sense of compassion in the heart).** Forgiveness is not the same as trust. Forgiveness should occur immediately; trust will likely have to be earned over time.

Forgiving Others

Hurting people hurt people. Maybe the hurt inflicted on you by another person was intentional; maybe it wasn't. The only thing to be certain of is that it hurt you. The hurt caused you to either move forward or become stagnated. Understand that you give the person who hurt you so much power in your life if you become stagnated. In most cases, the person inflicting the hurt has no idea how their actions have affected you–and may not even care. Remember, *hurting people hurt people*.

You say, 'I'll feel better if he/she apologizes or makes amends with me for the hurt they caused me, the way they treated me, the words they said to me....' Well, what if the apology never happens? Do you continue to lose precious moments of your life waiting for the apology? Or do you simply forgive them because you no longer want to be "stuck" rehearsing the act and the hurt associated with the act or the person? Do you see the power shift in the second option? By choosing (there's that submission principle again from Chapter 4) to forgive, the other person no longer has control over how you feel. You've taken your power/authority back.

"Forgiveness is unlocking the door to set someone free and...realizing you were the prisoner."

*Max Lucado*

Forgiving Yourself

The past. Sigh. Well, I'm not sure about you but there are certainly some things from my past that I wish I had not done or said. But I can't change the past and neither can you. I would like to challenge you to change your perspective about those things. Instead of continuing to carry these as burdens, let's choose to learn our lessons from them and allow those lessons to carry us to our blessings. Mistakes are a part of life's journey; they're inevitable. Learning lessons from them is so vital to our discovering our self-worth. Viewing mistakes as negatives hinders our ability to move forward to fully living and enjoying our life's plan. Choosing not to forgive ourselves also breeds anger, jealousy and even greed. It also makes it more difficult to sincerely forgive others.

Take a moment. Identify some of these past actions that you regret and may even feel guilty about. Really feel those emotions connected with them. It's okay to cry, shout, or even scream. It's okay. You've probably been carrying these with you for a long time. In some cases, you have probably allowed them to define you; to define your worth, especially the ones you kept repeating over and over and over again. Sister, you are not your past. You are not your mistakes. These were moments of preparation for the bigger plan at work in your life. Sister, YOU Matter!

*"You can clutch the past so tightly to your chest that it leaves your arms too full to embrace the present."*

***Jan Glidewell***

Forgiving God

So you are angry with God. This life you have...how in the world did He allow it? Why did He allow you to be mistreated, abused, assaulted, abandoned, raped, neglected, hurt, disappointed, suffer the death (or loss) of that special someone? It has you questioning if He really exists, doesn't it? It's okay to be angry. It's okay to be honest about it. Tell Him exactly how you feel. This is more about letting go of the unpleasant feelings associated with the lack of forgiveness that has accumulated in your heart. He already knows how you feel. He's God–He created you. He knows you better than you know yourself.

I've talked with so many women over the years. Quite a few of them have become skeptical of believing in God because of all of the evil that people do to each other, especially the bad things that have been done to them. A common question is, "If there is a God, why does He allow so much bad to happen?" My common response is something like this: "He gives us, human beings, the freedom of choice to do whatever we choose to do." Most don't like my response because it seems counterproductive that a Big, Mighty God who created the human being would then allow what He created to harm what He created; other human beings. I know. This is a difficult concept to grasp.

Remember, hurting people hurt people–that includes you and me. Do you realize that if other people did not hurt, the world would be a much different place in which to live? But I've come to accept that the hurt generates compassion. Compassion is a positive result of hurt. It's the ability to make something positive out of your pain (*the submission principle*). Who better to comfort a person than a person who's also endured the same and/or similar experience and/or life event? This is another one of those opportunities where we can take our influence back and use it positively to impact our part of the world.

**Sister, YOU Matter!**

> *"Don't let yesterday use up too much of today."*
> **Native American Proverb**

## Thankfulness/Gratefulness

> *"If you want to turn your life around, try thankfulness. It will change your life mightily."*
> **Gerald Good**

Thankfulness and gratefulness are important in maintaining our Crown because, without them, we will become dull and lose our contentment, our joy, and our serenity.

Thankfulness should be our essence. It should consume our being. It should be our attitude. This attitude shift will change our perspective about everything. Find at least one thing to be thankful for in ALL situations, even the ones that seem so awful. If we develop this attitude (and yes, this is a process) the awful times and experiences are not the focus; the good in those experiences will be.

Focusing on the good will make it much easier to get through the difficult experiences. For example, instead of focusing on the amount of money you don't have, focus on the thankfulness for the bills that have already been paid out of what you did earn. Even be grateful for the job that yielded the earnings. Instead of focusing on what we used to be, we can start focusing on where we are now and where we are headed; completing our assignment (remember that life plan I mentioned in Chapter 1?) When we do this, we begin to be thankful for second chances instead of mulling over the past mistakes, regrets, and missed opportunities.

 List five things for which you are thankful/grateful today.

1.

2.

3.

4.

5.

If you don't already, develop the practice of listing at least one thing for which you are grateful each day. This is a good listing to reference when you don't feel like there is anything going "right" in your life.

"Gratitude turns what we have into enough."

*Author Unknown*

## Humility

> *"There is nothing noble in being superior to your fellow man; true nobility is being superior to your former self."*
>
> **Ernest Hemingway**

I like the following portions of Webster's definition of humility: *"the state or quality of being humble; freedom from pride and arrogance; a modest estimate of one's own worth; a sense of one's own unworthiness through imperfection and sinfulness."*

Humility is important in our Crown maintenance routine because it keeps us grounded. It keeps us from comparing our Crown to the next woman's and thinking that our Crown is better and/or bigger because our past was different from hers. You know, it becomes so easy to act as if "we have arrived" when we think we have it all together. But Sister, it is only by grace and mercy that our walk is different from the next sister's walk. This should be the basis of our humility: "It could have been me." In all honesty, some of us are doing the same thing that we are criticizing and scrutinizing the next sister about–she just doesn't know our business and/or we haven't gotten caught doing what we do when we think no one else is looking. It's not our place to condemn our Sister. We have to treat our Sister the way we want to be treated, with love and compassion.

**Without humility, we will lose our goodness and gentleness (not needing to force our way in life.)**

> "People that put themselves above others will
> fall longer and harder."
>
> **Gina Lindley**

## Rest

> *"All relaxation does is allow the truth to be felt.*
> *The mind is cleared, like a dirty window wiped clean, and the*
> *magnitude of what we might ordinarily take for granted*
> *inspires tears."*
>
> **Jay Michaelson**

Rest is essential. It's a divine command. Without it, we cannot live life to its fullness. When we are functioning without the proper rest, we become irritable, prone to making careless mistakes and easily distracted. Even our bodies are affected. Our immune system is weakened, which makes us more susceptible to illnesses. Rest is "a period of inactivity, relaxation, mental or emotional calm; being motionless."(Freedictionary.com)

Rest is the ability to just let go, with no schedule, no extra "have to's." I envision rest as that lazy Saturday morning where there's absolutely nothing that **has** to be done. I can sleep in, or at least lie in bed a little longer. For those of us who work outside of the home or have young children, finding time to rest can be very challenging. Here is something I tried and it worked for me: I started completing some of the weekend chores during the week. For instance, I would begin laundry on

Thursday night instead of Friday night. On Friday nights, I would stay up late to complete the laundry chore. By the time I went to bed on Friday night (sometimes early Saturday morning), the clothing had been washed, folded, ironed and put away. It was one more chore that I did not have to complete on Saturday. I could use that time on Saturday to put my feet up or even watch a movie and not feel guilty about it.

Another lesson I learned regarding the chores: stop trying to have the perfect house all of the time, especially if you have younger children. Enjoy this valuable time with them. It goes by so fast and you can't get this time back--ever. Once it's gone, it's gone. Our children are young for a much shorter period of time in their lives than they are adults.

## Sleep

Although rest and sleep are commonly used interchangeably, they are not the same. However, sleep is very important. Did you know that it is even possible to sleep but not rest? When this happens, you generally experience the same effects of not getting enough sleep. Endless research studies have concluded that the average adult needs approximately 7-8 hours of sleep each night to restore the body with the energy it needs to handle all of the demands of living each day.

Research also suggests that there are many benefits to getting the recommended amounts of sleep each night. Some of these include that sleep: keeps your heart healthy; possibly prevents cancer; reduces stress and your risk for depression; increases your alertness and memory; may help you lose weight; and helps the body make repairs. (Stibich)

So now you may be asking the magical question: *How do I get 7-8 hours of sleep each night? My schedule is just too busy. Between the children, the husband, work, volunteer commitments, school, where do I find 7-8 hours for sleep/rest?* The answer is that you make it a priority. You schedule rest like you would that important meeting. Arrange your schedule around it. Now, there may be times when you can't stick to the schedule but this should be the exception and not the rule.

I will allow you to poke fun at me regarding this one technique. My family and friends know that if I am called after 9:00 p.m., they most likely will not talk to me. The ringer on the phone next to my bed is turned off. ALWAYS. I don't purchase a phone for my bedroom that will not allow me to turn the ringer off. Now, I'm good about returning calls the next day if a message is left but my friends and family know that they are "shooting in the dark" trying to get me on the phone after 9:00p.m., especially on a night before work. This was a very difficult transition for me but my day starts pretty early (4a.m.) and I learned–the hard way, of course–that I could not stay up late, which is my preference, and be productive the next day. So "9:00" is a running joke in my family. Go ahead, you can laugh, too.

**Rest is essential to maintaining patience, faithfulness and self-control.**

Now, let's look at some practical ways to include rest in your daily routine:

- ✓ Identify a sensible daily bedtime to allow the recommended 7-8 hours of sleep.
- ✓ Identify at least one day a week to rest (not sleep).
  - o If that seems impossible, identify at least 30 minutes a day.
  - o If that seems impossible, identify at least 15 minutes a day.

✓ Identify the tasks that consume your time.
  o Identify which of these are the essential tasks in your life.
    ▪ Examples: caring for your family (cooking, cleaning, etc.), going to work
  o Identify which of these are nonessential tasks in your life. Hint: These nonessential tasks can be traded for rest time.
    ▪ Examples: volunteer activities, watching television, social media surfing

"Your calm mind is the ultimate weapon against your challenges. So relax."

***Bryant McGill***
Simple Reminders: Inspiration for Living Your Best Life

*Sister, YOU Matter!*

# CONCLUSION

My Dear Sister, my hope is that you have been given the tools needed to coronate yourself and carry the regal air that accompanies your Crown. We have identified the components needed for your Crown and created your Crown. We have a better understanding of how to ensure that we our wearing our Crowns properly and coordinating our Crown with our many life roles. However, in all of our wearing, doing and being, be sure to maintain your Crown daily. Without the daily maintenance, your Crown's application and attributes will not be as effective as they need to be to help you accomplish your life's plan.

Sister, you already have it—your Crown. You just have to remember to embrace it and allow it to empower you to gain the place of authority and influence for which you are predestined.

Sister, YOU Matter so much and you are so essential. The world would not be the same without you. There would be a huge void without you.

Remember....

I Am the Crown!

I Am the Crown!

I am a human being.

I am a woman.

I am wonderfully created.

I am marvelously made.

I matter!

I Am the Crown!

www.sisterumatter.org

# SISTER, YOU MATTER!

## Works Cited

Adams, Rebecca. "This Is Why It's More Expensive to Be a Woman." *The Huffington Post*. TheHuffingtonPost.com. Web. 29Jan. 2015.

"Ancient Crowns (Bible History Online)." *Ancient Crowns (Bible History Online)*.Web.17 Dec. 2014.

"Bible Gateway." *The Message (MSG)*.Web. 1 Nov. 2014.

"Bible Gateway." *New Living Translation (NLT)*.Web. 30 Dec. 2015.

"Bing." *Commitment -*.Web. 30 Mar. 2015.

"Crown | Headwear." *Encyclopedia Britannica Online*. Encyclopedia Britannica.Web.17 Dec. 2014.

"Definition of Foundation in English:." *Foundation*.Web.8Mar. 2015.

"Dictionary, Encyclopedia and Thesaurus." *The Free Dictionary*. Farlex.Web. 30 Dec. 2015.

*Dictionary.com*. Dictionary.com. Web.1Nov. 2015.

"Grief Watch." *Symptoms of Grief*.Web.15Feb. 2015.

*Infoplease*. Info please. Web. 30 Dec. 2015.

*Merriam-Webster*.Merriam-Webster.Web.26Feb. 2015.

Osteen, Joel. "#439 - Being Pruned So You Can Bloom Pt 1." *YouTube*.YouTube.Web.1Feb. 2015.

Freudenrich, Ph.D. Craig."The Refining Process."*How Stuff Works*. HowStuffWorks.com. Web. 15Feb. 2015.

Stibich, Mark, PhD. "The 10 Reasons to Hit Your Pillow Early

Tonight." *About.com Health*. 16 Dec. 2014. Web.29Jan. 2015.

"Study Reveals the Average Woman Will Spend More of Her Life Wearing

Make-Up Than Not."*Beauty World News RSS*. 02 Feb. 2014. Web.29Jan.

2015.

"The Symbol of Power: The Top 10 Crowns in the World." *Swide Magazine the*

*Dolce Gabbana Luxury Magazine Online the Symbol of Power the Top 10*

*Crowns in the World Comments*. Web. 3 Nov. 2015.

# ABOUT THE AUTHOR

B.C. (Bakeba) Raines is an inspirational speaker, writer and the founder of Sister U Matter!®, a self discovery movement and awareness campaign. Her words and her passion for life has helped encourage many on their journey to learn how to embrace life. Her goal is to help women strive to be all they are purposed to be.

Bakeba resides in Montgomery, Alabama and is a mother, daughter, sister, and aunt who enjoys spending time with her family and friends. She also enjoys writing inspirational poems and article, baking and traveling.

To learn more about Bakeba and Sister U Matter!®, visit her website at www.bcraines.com or email her at info@bcraines.com

Made in the USA
Columbia, SC
11 April 2023

14683824R00081